The
Buckets *of* Money®
Retirement
Solution

"*Over the years I've sat across the desk from literally thousands of couples, business owners, retirees, and pre-retirees who have entrusted their financial well-being to me and my company. I take that responsibility very seriously, and that's why I wrote this book.* The Buckets of Money Retirement Solution *provides academically proven strategies that work in good times and in bad. It is a formula for a successful retirement, built on many years of hands-on experience with real people, real money, and real issues. Talking to people about their investments on the radio and TV, or writing about the subject in magazines may make for interesting listening, viewing, or reading, but there is so much more at stake when a family's financial future rests in your hands. For almost 40 years, I've been entrusted to help people find the right solution. I hope this book will help you make the first step on the path to a secure retirement with* The Buckets of Money Retirement Solution."

—Raymond J. Lucia CFP®

The
Buckets *of* Money®
Retirement Solution

THE ULTIMATE GUIDE TO INCOME FOR LIFE

Raymond J. Lucia, CFP®

with

Dale Fetherling

WILEY

John Wiley & Sons, Inc.

Published by John Wiley & Sons, Inc., Hoboken, New Jersey.
Published simultaneously in Canada.

Buckets of Money®, Bucketeer®, and Bucketize® are registered trademarks of Raymond J. Lucia Companies, Inc.

CFP® and Certified Financial Planner™ are registered trademarks of the Certified Financial Planner Board of Standards Inc.

For general information on our other products and services or for technical support, please contact our Customer Care Department within the United States at (800) 762-2974, outside the United States at (317) 572-3993 or fax (317) 572-4002.

Wiley also publishes its books in a variety of electronic formats. Some content that appears in print may not be available in electronic books. For more information about Wiley products, visit our web site at www.wiley.com.

Library of Congress Cataloging-in-Publication Data

Lucia, Raymond J.
  The buckets of money retirement solution : the ultimate guide to income for life / Raymond J. Lucia.
    p. cm.
  Includes index.
  ISBN 978-0-470-58157-5 (cloth); 978-0-470-90669-9 (ebk); 978-0-470-90670-5 (ebk); 978-0-470-90671-2 (ebk)
  1. Retirement income. 2. Finance, Personal. I. Title.
  HG179.L825 2010
  332.024'014—dc22
                                                            2010026713

Printed in the United States of America

10 9 8 7 6 5 4 3 2 1

To my loving wife,
Jeanne Lucia,
who has endured with consummate grace
both me and my years of seeking
the best retirement solutions for thousands of people
wanting to retire in comfort and safety.

Contents

Foreword

Try this on for size. You are having a test for the first 40 or so years of your work life. The test is on the subject of financial planning and getting your retirement right. If you pass the test, you get to live in a lovely home on a golf course or overlooking the lake, and you get to spend your days looking for your ball in the rough. At night you get to eat anywhere you want and then have a comfortable, secure, and restful sleep. You get to give money to your kids and grandkids and give them a leg up in life. You have the best medical care money can provide (Medicare is nowhere near comprehensive or free, by the way.) You cheerily and effortlessly pay your bills as they arrive. And you get to have the feeling you did something smart with your life. That's door one.

If you fail the test, you get to live in modest, cramped, noisy quarters. You get to worry about whether your wife is safe walking home from the Safeway. You get to feel sick when the monthly utility bill comes in the mailbox. You get to have to avoid creditors and juggle debts. You cannot sleep from fear and worry. And there is someone you cannot look in the eye when you get up in the morning and brush your teeth: yourself, because you know you screwed it up big time, this one and only life of yours. That's door two.

Which outcome would you like?

If it's door one, you would do well to take this book you now hold in your hands and take it to the cashier and buy it, go home, and start reading it and keep on until you are finished; then start the very next day doing what it says to do. Here's why I say this: I, your humble servant, have been following money matters since I was a teenager. That was roughly 50 years ago. In all of that time, I have never met anyone who knows the subject of personal finance as well as Ray Lucia. There are undoubtedly people who know more about monetary policy and some who know more about tariffs and trade. But on the subject of how to deploy your savings so that at the end of the day you are well taken care of, safe and secure, there is simply no one who is quite at the level of Raymond J. Lucia.

Ray has many insights: that you should arrange your investments to pay as little tax as possible. That you should diversify your stock market assets as widely as possible within the bounds of good sense. That you should make sure your money is in the hands of people who know more than you do. That you should be extremely cautious about leverage.

But he has one gigantic insight that tops all of these. It might be summarized thus: Stocks for the long run are the peerless investment. But we live not only in the long run but also in the short and medium run. In those runs, stocks can be crushingly disappointing and can ruin your life.

Yes, over multidecade periods, stocks outperform bonds and commodities and real property (at least in the postwar era). But in the short run, stocks can fall not only seriously, but calamitously. In periods of as long as a decade, stocks can have a zero or close to zero return. In periods of a few years, stocks can fall by 55 percent: we just saw it happen from the fall of 2007 to March of 2009. For those who had trusted in the stock market to always bring them out smiling, the days and nights were terrifying.

If families had bought at the top in 2007 in the stock market and desperately needed to cash out in late 2008 to March of 2009, they were devastated by their losses. The fear was tangible.

The genius—and that is not too strong a word—of Ray Lucia is that he saw all of this and had his investors "bucketized"—that is, had their savings in various different buckets of money—bonds, REITs, annuities, cash—such that they could ride out the stock market hurricane and get through to the daybreak.

Investors who trusted solely in stocks for the long run saw their hopes and dreams disappear, their confidence turn to terror. Investors who were "bucketized" never missed a moment's sleep. They did not do as well in the Great Recession as in boom times, but they had tiny losses and are back to solid gains as the stock markets have revived for now . . . and they are prepared to go through it again and again and always have high confidence that they will get through to the safe harbor.

That is Ray Lucia's great gift to his investors: he has them so diversified inside *and outside* the stock market that they can keep on trucking even in very bad times. He has the data to prove it.

You are probably skeptical, and you should be. Promises in the investment world are easy to make and hard to keep. But keep reading. If you can find the flaw in this investment concept, you are way ahead of me. Do not take it on trust. Read this. Then call or write to Ray and ask him for the data to back up his strategy. Analyze the data, and compare it with any metrics you choose. You will be amazed at how sound Ray's plan is.

It really takes diversification to a level of caution and prudence one rarely sees. Ray takes you to a state of caution that is, sadly, desperately needed in the real world of financial slips, falls, scoundrels, and poor governance. It is a level rarely achieved by money managers. And you need that level. But, again, don't take my word for it. Read this and see how it works for you. And if you find a better way to invest, go for it. You won't hurt my feelings. In fact, I want to hear about it. I might put it this way: If you can find a way to stay afloat in water by yourself indefinitely without a life jacket, let me know. Ray's ideas are the life jacket.

But you'll never know how well it works unless you keep reading. And remember: door one or door two?

—BEN STEIN

Acknowledgments

My family has been the heart and soul of my company, and the inspiration behind my professional pursuits since I went into the financial services industry almost 40 years ago. It is to them—and also to our extended family of friends, associates and advisors we have been graced with through the years—that this book is dedicated.

I would like to express my deepest gratitude and enduring love to my wife of 37 years, Jeanne, who has been by my side for all the best moments of my life. Jeanne is the matriarch of the family, who has nurtured it through the generations with her grace and kindness.

To my eldest son, Ray Jr., who recently became President and CEO of RJL Wealth Management. While I'm proud to have founded Raymond J. Lucia Companies, a very successful investment management and financial planning firm, I'm even more proud of Ray Jr's leadership, his accomplishments, and his potential to guide RJL Wealth Management toward a bright and prosperous future. In his hands, and under the direction of his brilliant mind, he will be more than a custodian of my professional legacy, he will be an innovator that will shape the industry for generations to come.

To my children, Alana and Dom, who work alongside me every day. Their choice to join my company gave me the proximity to my kids that other parents can only dream of. And to my daughter, Niki, who inherited the artistic aspect of her father's genetic code; her passion and creativity are inspiring.

To my big brother, Joe, who has worked tirelessly alongside me and has stood by me through every trial and tribulation. Joe embodies the spirit and personality of the company we've built together.

To my nephew, Joey, who leads by example with his commitment and organizational skills, and has proven himself to be one of the sharpest minds in the industry.

To the Brain Trust, the talented team I work with every day on my radio show: Rick Plum, the smartest CFP in the country; Rob

Butterfield, the most knowledgeable tax attorney on the planet; and John Dean, the best radio producer and foil a talk show host could ever have . . . those three hours a day are truly priceless.

To Melissa Dotson, who has worked with me from Day One, and continues to be a valued and trusted partner after almost 40 years together. To Trina Jensen, my executive assistant, who makes every day easier for me because of her reliability and thoroughness.

To each of the *Buckets of Money* advisors, for their diligence in learning and studying the strategy, and having the discipline to consistently implement it on behalf of every client they serve.

To our profound colleague, advisor, and sage, Ben Stein, an unparalleled mind in the world of finance and economics. It is truly an honor to have you as a confidant, and as a part of the family.

Finally, this book is dedicated to my parents, whom I'm still blessed to have in my life. I hope we're all making you proud of what we've accomplished, and more importantly, of the kind of people who you've shaped us to become.

Introduction

LET'S GET YOUR FUTURE BACK ON TRACK

It's long been said that a rising tide lifts all boats. But the financial tsunami that hit us in 2007–2008 seemingly sent all vessels to the bottom—stocks, bonds, commodities, real estate . . . you name it! Almost no investment was left unscathed. And if you're like most of the people I talk to, you may feel as if your retirement plan has run totally aground. How will you possibly get afloat again?

Many workers and retirees have lost confidence in their ability to fund or enjoy a financially secure retirement. In fact, according to a recent survey by the Employee Benefit Research Institute, just 13 percent of workers claim to be "very confident" about having enough money for retirement. That's the lowest percentage of workers feeling that way since EBRI first began asking the question 15 years ago. What's worse, some 44 percent of workers are either "not at all" or "not too" confident about attaining that secure retirement.

Such a drop in confidence isn't hard to understand. The average retirement account lost a third of its value—and often more—in calendar 2008. In fact, the last couple of years have been among the toughest in history for investors. Once-proud companies like Lehman Brothers, Citigroup, GM, AIG, and Chrysler have gone belly-up or nearly so, and many others struggle. Government intervention has reached epic levels. Headlines often have been bleak, and selling at times seemed to be indiscriminate.

So whether you were loading up on stocks to fund a long retirement, trading online to time the market, or even relying on a buy-and-hold strategy, you probably lost a lot. What's more, many people saw the value of their retirement assets fall even as their debt rose. And in too many cases, their jobs were lost or replaced with lower-paying ones.

"By year end," as Warren Buffett so colorfully stated, "investors of all stripes were bloodied and confused, much as if they were small birds that had strayed into a badminton game." So it's not surprising that another recent survey, this one by Bank of America, found that more than half of respondents planned to change their investment strategy. And that's good. But it begs the question: Change it to *what?*

A New Strategy?

Well, you could start investing with Bernard Madoff and get his consistently high returns in good years and bad. *Whoops!* Scratch that. That option is no longer operative, as they used to say in politics. Or, you could plunge into, say, tech stocks . . . *whoops!* again. We all saw that movie several years ago.

Then there's real estate. Well, maybe not. You've also likely seen your home equity shrink. If you were lucky, you avoided foreclosure or a short sale, but even so you can be forgiven for lacking a lot of confidence in the real estate market these days.

Or . . . here's an idea: How about gold? A lot of people are talking up gold as if we're entering a new Dark Ages from which only guns, stockpiles of canned food, and hoarded amounts of the yellow metal will save us. Magazine covers, TV commercials, and the guy down the street—they're all beating the drums for owning gold—gold coins, gold-mining companies, gold bullion . . . almost anything that glitters.

But if you do a little study you'll see it's clear that a little gold goes a long way.

As an investment, gold's average annualized returns have only barely kept up with inflation. Folks who bought gold 30 years ago are just now getting their money back.

The Fickle Fads

In fact, you probably want to avoid *any* hot trend. I was thinking just the other day about how fickle financial fads can be. In my experience, the more chatter and the more hype, the more likely some bubble is just about to burst.

Think about it. When your neighbors are bragging about their soaring home equity, falling home prices are probably just around the corner. When your auto mechanic wants to share stock tips, you can bet a bear market looms. When everyone's atwitter about dotcoms . . . well, you remember that era and know how that one ended.

My strong advice—be wary of the latest investing trend, whatever it is. Usually by the time word of it hits the mainstream media or becomes the buzz at the local café, that asset has already peaked and is about to plummet. The truth is, financial publications, the mainstream press, and the population at large is almost uniformly wrong about the timing of the newest cutting-edge investment opportunity. (Magazine covers, for instance, are infamous for being "contrary indicators." Perhaps the most celebrated example is a 1979 *BusinessWeek* cover heralding "The Death of Equities." Soon after it appeared, a roaring 20-year bull market in stocks began.)

Stick with Cash?

Okay, you say, if a lot of the much-touted investment ideas don't measure up long-term, then maybe the best thing is to just stay with cash. Put it in the bank, in money market accounts, in Treasury bills, under the mattress or buried in an old Mason jar . . . *somewhere?*

No-o-o. That's also bad. For one thing, there's a real possibility of high inflation in the coming years. And even modest inflation eats away at what your cash can buy. Even with inflation at 3 percent (which is *much* lower than many predict), the purchasing power of a dollar is cut in half in a little more than 23 years. Yes, you'd still have your greenbacks in, say, 20 years. But, no, they very well may not buy enough of what you'll need in retirement.

But I sense what some of you may be thinking: "What if I just stash my cash, then get back in the stock market when the next upturn begins?" That sounds good. But it's not good, sound reasoning. Nobody's that smart. There's an old saying, "They don't ring a bell when the market hits a bottom" (or, for that matter, a top). In other words, nobody can pinpoint when stocks will take off.

And often the start of the upswing is sudden and sharp. (On average, the S&P 500 has risen 38.1 percent in the first 12 months after the end of a bear market, according to the respected research firm Ibbotson Associates.) So when that upswing occurs, you don't want to be left behind earning, say, 1 percent or 2 percent in a savings account or have all your money locked up in Treasury bonds.

My recommendation: Don't let the present turmoil and uncertainty lead you to do something you'll regret. Unless you're independently wealthy, you probably need stocks to meet your long-term investment objectives. And you'll most likely need to own them when you're least likely to want them. Take, for example, early March 2009. Then it seemed as if everyone loathed the stock market, which had plummeted more than 50 percent from its high. In fact, many fools pulled out of the market then, determined never to be burned again. However, they left as much as 70 percent returns on the table as the market went on to post its best rally since 1933.

What Else Is There?

"But, Ray," you're probably saying, "if I can't effectively time the market and I can't just sit on cash, if real estate is fluky and precious metals are unreliable, and if just buying and holding stocks hasn't worked out, what in the world should I do?"

I'm glad you asked that. Because that's what this book is about: helping you chart a course out of your financial shipwreck. I'm going to give you a strategy that's battle-tested and time-tested, tested in fact in more than 9,000 individual portfolios totaling more than $2 billion. It's been proven, hands down, to be the best way to safeguard your retirement holdings. Yes, it involves the stock market but also other kinds of assets as well. And the key is how you allocate those assets and how to choose to draw them down to finance your sunset years.

Time-Tested Principles

I had a caller to my radio show tell me the other day that some experts are saying the next 10 or 20 years will be a downer for stocks. "So," he asked, "isn't it folly to be in the market at all?"

Well, what I told him was if you find a dozen so-called experts, you may get a dozen opinions. For instance, a few years ago, one well-known "economic futurist" wrote a best-selling book predicting the Dow would hit 44,000 by 2008. We now know he was off by about 34,000 points.

The truth is, neither you, I, nor anyone else can accurately predict the next 20 years. But we have a choice: We can follow time-tested investment principles, or we can fly by the seat of our pants (or by the seat of some guru's pants). I think both you and I know which of those is the better option.

When there's a stock market meltdown, such as in 2008, a lot of investors say, "That's it. I'll never invest in stocks again." Some flail around wildly, others panic or go catatonic. But the wisest course is to come up with a strategy and execute it as fully and calmly as possible. The results will likely surprise you. And this book aims to give you that strategy. It's a strategy designed to help shield you from the short-term ups and downs of the market. It can give you the courage and discipline to stay invested no matter what the future holds and thus let you plan your retirement years with greater confidence.

How This Book Unfolds

Filled with examples and what I believe are clear, specific calculations, the book unfolds in four parts: First, you'll be encouraged to regain your balance as the first two chapters explain the changing financial landscape and how to prepare for whatever the economic future holds. In the second section, three chapters explain in detail the *Buckets of Money* plan, including how to choose the proper investments and execute the strategy.

The third section offers refinements on that plan. Specifically, it details how annuities, real estate investment trusts, personally-owned real estate, and taxes can come into play in your *Buckets of Money* plan. And, finally, the fourth and last section explains how to create a workable withdrawal strategy once your plan is in place and working.

An epilogue then tops off the book with a favorite theme of mine: how to keep all this money stuff in perspective by making sure your retirement is filled as well with people and interesting pursuits. Enjoy!

The Importance of a Plan

Just doing nothing and hoping your financial situation will improve doesn't work. That's because, as I like to say, hope is a virtue, but it's not a strategy. Which reminds me of an old joke: A guy dies and goes to heaven where he confronts God. "Hey," he says, "couldn't you have at least let me win the lottery?" God replies: "Couldn't *you* have at least bought a lottery ticket?"

The point is that doing nothing and just hoping things will get better really won't hack it. You've got to come up with a plan. And the one I'm going to give you—the *Buckets of Money* plan—is the best idea I've developed (or seen anyone else develop) over my more than 30 years of being a financial advisor.

Here, in barest essence, is how it works: Put your money into three piles, or "buckets," and invest each in a different way. Bucket 1, the Income bucket, contains safe, low-growth vehicles like CDs, money markets, Treasuries, life annuities, or short-term bonds or bond funds. Drawing down both principal and interest from this bucket provides a stable income stream for a certain period of time.

Bucket 2, the Relative Safety bucket, is invested only slightly more aggressively and holds assets such as mid-term bonds, Treasury Inflation-Protected Securities, mortgage-backed securities, fixed and indexed annuities, and corporate and municipal bonds. When Bucket 1 is depleted, empty Bucket 2 into it for another specified number of years. Meanwhile, Bucket 3, the Growth bucket—reserved largely for real estate, stocks, and alternative investments—continues to have time to grow.

By the time Bucket 1 is depleted for the second time, Bucket 3—if the stock market and real estate meet historical norms—should provide a nice chunk of change to allow you to rebucketize and see yourself through your retirement years.

This plan gives you the courage and the discipline to take advantage of the historically proven growth in long-term investments. All in all, this plan is akin to a sports car that seats six, approximating the best of both worlds—in this case by being a conservative strategy that's also growth-oriented.

Of course, lots of variations and refinements exist, and we'll soon get into all those. But the important thing with the *Buckets of Money* plan is that as you grow older others may have to make do with less and less, but you—having mastered this strategy—will potentially be growing stronger and more secure. You'll be able to sleep at night because you'll be following the science of money, not the art of speculation.

My Bias

Before I get into the nitty–gritty of this strategy, though, let me give you a sense of where I'm coming from. Yes, I'm a CFP, or Certified Financial Planner professional. I'm the founder of Raymond J. Lucia Companies, Inc., the predecessor of RJL Wealth Management, a highly successful investment-management and financial planning firm, RJL Wealth Management (run by my son Ray Jr., a CPA). In fact, I've spent most of my adult life helping people safely retire.

I've been in the financial services industry for more than three decades. I'm the host of a nationally syndicated money talk show and have, in conjunction with all the advisors with whom I've worked, invested some $2 billion on behalf of about 9,000 clients.

I read obsessively on financial matters and talk to a lot of people on my radio show and at seminars. But I'm not a finance professor, nor do I consider myself an expert researcher by any means. My particular expertise lies more in the practical realm of dealing with real people retiring and investing their money strategically so their bank account doesn't expire before they do.

My bias is that I like *facts*, not pontification. And I like hard numbers, not abstractions. And that's what I'm going to try to give you as I explain this strategy. This sets me apart from a lot of people in the financial field. In fact, let me tell you a story that will make the point.

Not long ago I was on a panel discussion with Ben Stein, the writer/economist/actor, and two other economists. These other two guys, though probably quite brilliant, were talking well over everyone's head, including mine. I could tell Ben also was becoming very frustrated with their lengthy and technical answers to relatively easy, straightforward questions. And I could barely get a word in edgewise.

Finally, a young lady in the back of the room stepped up to the microphone and asked a question of the panel: "I'm 25 years old," she said, "and I'm wondering with the Social Security system going broke, will my husband and I ever be able to afford to retire?" For me, this type of question is a big, fat pitch right over the plate.

But before I could answer, one of the economists to my left beat me to the punch and began a dissertation about how many working people theoretically will be required 40 years from now to support her Social Security payments. Then the economist to *his* left began arguing with him about the politics of the Social Security system. Ben was fidgeting in his chair, disgusted with their lack of attention to the simple question: Will she and her husband be able to retire?

Finally, a split second of silence appeared, so I jumped in.

"Young lady," I asked, "how old did you say you and your husband are?"

"Twenty-five."

"And when would you like to retire?"

"Age 55 or so," she replied.

I went on, "I don't think you can count on maximizing your Social Security benefits until at least age 70. You see, the system as it stands today will be able to fund about 70 percent of your promised benefits, but not 100 percent. So while Social Security is not totally broke, the benefits will have to be cut or taxes increased or some combination of those two unpopular choices. I suspect we will see the Social Security normal-retirement age gradually increase from age 67 to age 72 or so by the time you're ready to receive it. It's a way to cut benefits without saying you're cutting benefits."

I heard Ben say under his breath, "That's exactly correct."

I continued, "So, as I said, the system isn't totally broke; it's about one-third broke. Nonetheless, let's pretend you will have no Social Security at all. Tell me, if you were to retire today, how much income will the two of you need to live on for the rest of your lives?"

"About $50,000 per year," she said.

"And how much have you saved for your retirement so far?"

"Seventy-five thousand," she exclaimed.

"And how much are you and your husband saving, including company matching contributions in your 401(k)s, IRAs and other pensions?"

"About $25,000 per year."

"That's fantastic," I replied. Now as a CFP professional and retirement planner I never go anywhere without my wonderful HP12C calculator. It enables me to do present value and amortization calculations right on the spot—and I've become quite proficient at its use. As I listened to her answers, I entered her data into my calculator.

"Well let's see," I said, "if inflation averages 3 percent annually and you want to retire in 30 years on $50,000 per year, you'll need about $121,000 to buy then what $50,000 buys today." She was in shock, yet amazed at my speedy calculations.

"And if you and your husband have a joint life expectancy of, say, 40 years post-retirement, you'll need about $2.8 million saved up by then to pay you that $121,000 inflation-adjusted income for life. That's the bad news," I said.

"The good news is that you have $75,000 already saved and you are saving $25,000 per year. If you do that consistently for the next 30 years and earn 7.5 percent or 8 percent on your money, you will have amassed $3.2 million to $3.5 million. That's enough for you to retire whether you get Social Security or not. So, the answer to your question is, 'Yes, you and your husband can probably retire at 55, and any Social Security payments you receive will be an added bonus.'"

She was relieved, thanked me profusely and eased back to her seat. Ben, without any hesitation, looked at me, and jabbing his index finger at me in the best Robert De Niro imitation he could muster, said, "You, you're *good*!"

That's what I do. I try to give people very specific answers. And that's what I will do in this book.

The
Buckets *of* Money®
Retirement
Solution

PART I

REGAIN YOUR BALANCE

CHAPTER

1

Adapt to the Changing Landscape

In cartoons, when a boulder falls and drives a character into the ground, he's briefly stunned. We laugh at his frazzled look and empathize with his despair. But soon he shakes off the hurt, his flattened head returns to normal, and all is well. So we laugh some more. Trouble is, I don't think this last recession is like that.

The boulder that fell on us in 2007–2008 is likely to change the face of investing and retirement planning for a long time, perhaps forever. The market meltdown and the ensuing government response are reshaping the financial landscape. Old ways of thinking about retirement are going out the window. New ideas are called for.

In this chapter, I'm going to outline some of the changes we've seen, or are likely to see, and explain how I think they'll affect retirement planning in general. In the following chapter, I'll get more specific about how this could, or should, affect *your* planning.

The End of Easy

Whatever else you call the recent economic convulsion—the "Great Recession," a "severe downturn," or "the worst financial crisis since 1929"—it's what many have labeled "the End of Easy." The end of getting a mortgage without having to show you can repay it. The end of inflation that's so low it's barely perceptible. The end of government that takes a hands-off stance toward business. The end of relentlessly soaring home prices that make houses into virtual ATMs. And probably pretty much the end of the idea that you're going to be able to get by on a guaranteed company pension and Social Security.

A new reality has been brewing for several decades and has accelerated during the recent unpleasantness. And here's the bottom line: *More than ever, you're going to be on your own.* Being on your own and acting wisely on financial matters isn't the easiest thing to do, especially if you have a job, a family, and a mortgage. And, of course, for those who've lost their jobs, the challenge is of a whole other order of magnitude. So more than ever, you'll need to do some hard thinking about the future.

Let's look at some of these tectonic shifts in the economic landscape as they affect retirement:

- **Houses aren't what they used to be.** Until recently, about the only qualifying test for getting a home loan was the ability to fog a mirror. If you could breathe, you could probably get the money. Even if the monthly payment was more than you could afford, that would be okay because the market value presumably would soon soar, then you could refinance, take on an even bigger debt and end up with a wad of cash in your pocket and bragging rights about your house's astronomical value.

  It was like musical chairs. Everyone was moving on and moving up . . . but then the music stopped. Suddenly, almost anyone who'd bought a house in the past few years owed more than it was worth. Foreclosures and short sales soared. The home-building industry collapsed. Millions of people lost their homes. Many preretirees who'd been counting on their home equity to fund their sunset years were dealt a huge blow.

- **Many investors lost confidence in stocks.** From its peak in October 2007 to early March 2009, the Standard & Poor's 500–stock index fell more than 56 percent. The decline was so severe that it brought down long-term performance figures, too. In fact, Ibbotson Associates' figures show that the market's horrific performance in 2008 and early 2009, coming on top of the 2000–2002 downturn, makes this one of the worst decades ever for stocks. Annualized total return after inflation actually was worse (–5.8 percent) for the 10-year period ending in February 2009 than the annualized total return (–5.0 percent) for the 10 years ending in August 1939.

Even with the stunning stock-market rally beginning in March 2009, the S&P 500 still posted a negative return for the decade.

Net *inflows* into stock funds in February 2007, before equities peaked, were $27 billion. Two years later, the net *outflow* for February 2009 was $25 billion, according to the Investment Company Institute, a mutual-fund trade group.

So investors can be forgiven for feeling a bit bewildered. All the oft-recited statistics about stocks averaging 8 to 10 percent annual gains long-term proved, at least for the past decade, to be a cruel joke. (As I've stated many times, "long term" should mean 15 to 25 years. That's because every so often, we have "a lost decade" in which stocks go nowhere. Of course, no one knows when that next will happen.) So while some investors are looking for beaten-down stocks in order to take advantage of a hoped-for rally, many others are unlikely to shake off the recent collapse so quickly: The mind-set that they'd worked under for the past 20 or so years has been dented.

- **Feelings of economic insecurity are rampant.** Confusion reigns. The sharp drop in equities has made even the wealthy feel more pessimistic and risk-averse, according to recent surveys. Fidelity polled some 1,000 millionaires and found 46 percent of them were less than comfortable with their financial positions. And in its tenth year, the Phoenix Wealth Survey, conducted by Harris Interactive, found that of 1,700 respondents, 30 percent were downbeat, six times the proportion who felt that way in 2000.

   Some 50 percent of the millionaires talking to Phoenix said they were unsure exactly how to invest. That compares with 32 percent in 2008 and 26 percent in 2007 who felt that way.
- **"Defined-benefit" pensions are on the way out.** Our parents and grandparents worked decades for the same companies because their pension plans promised a secure retirement. Those days are largely over.

   As recently as 1985, according to the Labor Department, about 80 percent of employees in medium-sized and large companies had such plans, which promise a lifetime stipend. But by 2000, defined-benefit recipients had dwindled to just 36 percent. What's happened is that employees were saddled with the investment and actuarial risks as their employers shifted to "defined contribution" formulas. The result is that many employers now contribute to 401(k) plans that are managed by the employees. Unfortunately, as we'll soon see, workers often don't do a very good job of managing those investments.

What's more, with the recession slamming profits, many of the remaining company pension plans are underfunded. The Pension Benefit Guaranty Corp., which underwrites private pensions, recently reported its largest deficit ever. And Congress, seeking to prevent retirees from draining badly needed cash from the plans, is requiring pension plans to restrict lump-sum payouts when any plan is less than 80 percent funded. At that point, workers can receive only half of the amount in a lump sum, with the other half as an annuity. Plans that are less than 60 percent funded can provide no lump sums, only annuities. That adds up to another curveball tossed at soon-to-be retirees who were counting on a big windfall.

- **Meanwhile, "defined contribution" plans have lost some of their luster.** Many 401(k) and similar plans suffered a loss of nearly 50 percent in value—peak to trough—over the past year or two. This has imperiled retirement for older workers and led some younger workers to wonder whether they should participate at all.

When 401(k)-type plans came on the scene in the early 1980s, they were viewed mainly as supplements to employer-funded pension and profit-sharing plans. Because 401(k) participants were presumed to have their basic retirement-income security needs covered by an employer-funded plan and Social Security, they were given substantial discretion over 401(k) choices. In a sense, everyone was encouraged to become an investment expert.

Now, many firms are cutting back—at least temporarily—on their contributions.

And because of the recession and the fact that many 401(k)s haven't been well-managed by their holders, the balances in those plans likely will be insufficient as the sole supplement to Social Security.

In fact, the Congressional Research Service (CRS) did a study on consumer finances and found that for the 53 percent of households that hold at least one retirement account, the median combined balance was $45,000. Of course, that includes younger workers who haven't yet started saving a lot.

But for households headed by persons between the ages of 55 and 64, the median value of all retirement accounts was just $100,000. Better, huh? Well, sure, but that amount would buy an annuity paying perhaps $700 a month for life, based on current interest rates. And how many lattes is that going to buy you in, say, 20 years?

To make matters worse, the CRS study was based on consumer-finance figures gathered by the Federal Reserve in 2007—*before* the market meltdown. So the median account balances likely are a good deal lower now.

- **Our savings and investing habits have been slow to change.** In recent decades, Americans have become the consummate consumers. Savers, not so much. According to the Commerce Department's Bureau of Economic Analysis, the national savings rate was about 11 percent in 1981. Before the recent meltdown, it fell to about 1.7 percent and has since rebounded to roughly 3 percent. Personal bankruptcies are rising. We're still credit-card addicts.

Hewitt Associates recently released a study showing that despite record losses in 401(k) accounts in 2008, savings and investing habits barely budged. The median 401(k) plan balance dropped from $79,600 in 2007 to $57,200 by the end of 2008. Yet the vast majority of workers continued to save in their plan at roughly the same rate. Fewer than one in five workers, Hewitt said, made any trade in their 401(k) in 2008.

Fidelity didn't do a survey but instead relied on actual behavior among the more than 11 million participants in the pension programs it runs. Fidelity's numbers indicated that only about one of every 29 plans participants traded out of one fund and into another in their plan. Such a low level of activity suggests that investors for the most part are sticking with the investment strategy they started with, which may well be a plan that's no longer suitable or appropriate.

Active trading rarely makes sense. But adjusting the amount you save or rebalancing your portfolio from time to time is prudent and advisable.

- **Credit is getting a lot harder to get.** Banks have put the squeeze on all kinds of consumer loans. The bar has been raised on who gets the very best rates. Lenders are ratcheting up minimum credit scores, requiring bigger down payments, and upping interest rates for borrowers with less-than-perfect credit histories. In other words, to get a loan you now need to be financially fit and have the documents to prove it.

  As far as mortgages are concerned, lenders are eying an overall debt-to-gross income ratio that falls below 40 percent—that's down from the 55 percent or 60 percent that some lenders would approve before the mortgage meltdown. Even if a lender does not hold you to this standard, you'd be smart to do so yourself. Plus, down payments are back in vogue. Plan on putting down at least 10 percent, though 20 percent will get you a better rate. And you'll need the paperwork to prove your income, assets, and overall balance sheet.

  Also, expect tougher financing for cars and say good-bye to no-cash-down deals. Lenders are also restricting the lengths of auto loans. So signing up for a loan that's longer than five years—a common practice until recently—may not be an option.

  Credit-card companies are reducing credit limits, raising interest rates and fees, and closing idle accounts in response to rising business costs and charge-offs, which occur when banks treat delinquent accounts as a loss. Days of a $25,000 credit limit based on a credit score in the 600s are largely gone. And getting approved for a new credit card is definitely getting more difficult.

- **Tax hikes—maybe really big ones—are in the offing.** Total federal debt almost doubled during President George W. Bush's administration, and as much as we needed stimulus spending by the Obama administration to boost the economy, the nonpartisan Congressional Budget Office now estimates total debt levels could almost double again over the next eight years, with our "tax bill doubling over time." Excessive debt virtually guarantees our taxes are going up, way up.

  Funding for Medicare and Social Security, as you've probably read, present real challenges. Those two trust funds already eat up more than a third of the federal budget and increase by $2 trillion each year. Medicare surpluses will run out in 2016. Social Security will be spending more than it takes in by 2017 and will be broke by 2037.

- **Inflation predicted.** Inflation rose an average of 3.3 percent over the past 25 years, according to the Bureau of Labor Statistics index that tracks the cost of living for those age 62 or older. (That index weighs prices for medical care and shelter more heavily than does the overall inflation index.) But, pessimists warn, printing a lot of money will lead to runaway inflation.

The Lessons

What are we to draw from all this? What does this most recent grizzly bear of the market tell us? It tells us that when markets go down as much as they did in 2008–2009, it's easy to:

- **Suffer paralysis by analysis . . . and end up doing nothing.** Just keep doing what you've always been doing, and you'll probably end up with the same results.

    The research firm Dalbar, Inc., has found that while the S&P 500 index earned an average of 8.4 percent during the 20 years through 2008, the average individual investor earned an annual return of just 1.9 percent. That's because many investors followed their emotions and tended to jump in and out of stocks.
- **Get mad, point fingers, and swear off investing forever.** Nor is this a very good strategy. Those investors who will survive and thrive will be those who can keep their heads and also use those heads. In other words, you don't want to overreact, but you also don't want to hide your head in the sand and refuse to adapt to the new reality. You want to figure out what you did wrong and fix it.

    Clearly, Americans are going to need to try harder to live within their means. That entails creating a budget and sticking with it. It means calculating retirement expenses as carefully as possible. It means rebuilding your savings, rethinking your retirement years, and retooling your retirement-savings plans, all of which will be covered in the next chapter. You've also got to invest differently, which I'll explain after that.

A Final Word

The recent "Great Recession" revealed some major changes in our economic landscape. People came to see that their homes can't be infinite sources of income, for example, that the economic security that their parents or grandparents may have enjoyed may be a thing of the past, and that our savings and investing habits need to change. The question then becomes this: What can you do about that? In the next chapter we'll talk about how you can adjust your individual situation to make the most of these new realities.

CHAPTER

2

Prepare for Whatever the Future Holds

Despite some recent gains in the stock market, portfolios remain badly wounded by events of the last couple of years. Jobs are still disappearing at a rapid rate, the recession remains a serious concern, and policymakers continue to implement unprecedented—and unprecedentedly expensive—solutions. No one knows how this is all going to turn out.

But, then, we *never* do. Life—and investing—are always uncertain. But in troubled times like these, you can take steps to situate yourself for whatever the long term will bring.

Yes, these are unsettled—even scary—economic times. But even within those financial clouds silver linings can be found, and action can be taken. Stocks experienced some of their most robust years ever in the midst of the Great Depression. After falling 86 percent at the outset, the market then surged 54 percent in 1933, 48 percent in 1935, and 34 percent in 1936.

So, particularly if you're young with decades before retirement, 2008 may have handed you a wonderful gift. That's because you can scoop up investments and houses at rock-bottom prices.

If you're 50 or older, you may need to work a few years longer than you planned. But that'll give you time to replenish your savings, delay claiming Social Security benefits until they're worth more later, and give your investments time to recover. And even if you're retired or about ready to retire, you can look at other steps, such as adjusting your withdrawal rate and maybe seeking part-time work. And shun panic selling. After all, you won't need all your money at once.

We'll get into all of those possibilities. But, first, whatever your retirement horizon, this chapter will outline some of the moves you can make that will give you a leg up should the recovery take longer than expected or, heaven forbid, if we were to be hit soon again by another economy-shattering external event or severe financial setback.

Here's how I see these steps in broad strokes:

1. Rebuild your savings.
2. Rethink your retirement years.
3. Retool your retirement savings plans.
4. Reinvent your strategy.

Once we've surveyed the nuts and bolts of these moves, you should be able to have a good grasp of the needed decisions that'll help form the broad boundaries of your overall retirement. Then we'll jump into the specifics of the *Buckets of Money* plan—specifics that I believe should be at the heart of how you invest your money to make those broad plans come true.

Rebuild Your Savings

Saving is now cool—and critical. Extravagance is out, frugality is in. However, this will not be an easy transition for some folks.

A lot of our financial problems over the past couple years can be traced to an absence of clear thinking. A good starting point to avoiding that is to remember what Rudyard Kipling wrote: Keep your head about you when everyone else is losing theirs.

For instance, viewing housing and the stock market as never-can-lose gambits or spending far more than we have—these fall into the category of muddled thinking. It's also that kind of murky thinking that's a boon to fraudsters, allowing them to snooker investors.

It's a great temptation in tough times to think that things will never get better. But history shows us things do eventually improve. And, in fact, this downturn appears to be slowing, if not reversing, as policymakers strive to find solutions. So, brighter times loom. Until then, try to get your thinking and your saving back on track as well as aim to eliminate your high-cost debt and get on a budget.

Clearly, you must save for retirement. You want to make sure you live in a home you can afford and enjoy. And you need to reject get-rich schemes. In short, be prudent, save money, invest wisely. Get back to the basics, rebuild your savings and your portfolio, and plan for a better day. Most people who've amassed wealth did it the hard way: They deferred spending in order to save for tomorrow.

Finding "fat" to cut probably isn't going to be that tough. For instance, households making more than $70,000 per year spent $4,600 each on restaurant food in 2007, according to the Bureau of Labor Statistics, and the average couple spends $3,000 a year on leisure travel. But if you could, say, give up one or both of those indulgences, you could help unscramble your nest egg.

Saving a few dollars here or there can add up, especially if you stash the money in a high-interest-bearing savings account, say, or a tax-favored vehicle like an IRA containing a mix of investments offering high potential returns over the long term.

So, specifically, what *can* you do?

Practically speaking, how can you live well on less in a tough economy? For starters, you may want to adjust your attitude. No amount of anger or blame (at yourself or others) is going to restore your investment losses. But what will help is moving forward with a concrete plan. Focus on the things you can control to help you get back on the right track, no matter your age or how close you are to retiring.

Here are some ideas to get your started:

- **Trim your debts.** Unlike fine wine (or my wife Jeanne), debts don't improve with age. If there's a single financial lesson to be learned from the past few years, it's this: *Don't Overdo the Debt.* Shakespeare's "Neither a borrower nor a lender be" rarely has seemed more fitting.

  Too many of us overextended ourselves during the past decade with credit cards and other debt. The average household has roughly $11,000 worth of credit-card debt with an average interest rate of 14 percent. That's ridiculously costly.

  So the first order of business is to eliminate—or, at least, reduce—this expensive debt, even before saving for retirement or investing. As you save money, using perhaps some of the following techniques, you should devote the savings to eliminating your credit-card debt.

- **Get on a budget.** Thrift is fashionable again. Getting on a budget means measuring exactly what you spend and looking for ways to save money. Several fine web sites exist—such as Mint .com, Quicken.com, and Wesabe.com—that can help you sort out your spending and a give you a sense of where you can save. You can upload password information for your credit cards and other accounts, and let the sites aggregate and sort the data. That way you'll see how much you're spending on, for instance, eating out or on clothes. Then you can track your spending habits over time and make needed changes.

- **Continue saving for retirement.** Ours has been dubbed the YOYO Era, meaning *"You're On Your Own."* And in tough times, we tend to focus on our immediate threat: mainly, getting the current bills paid. But we're all still going to want to retire at some point, so it's important to remain disciplined about saving for that eventuality.

  The 401(k) system rewards consistent saving and patient, long-term investing.

  Employer-sponsored 401(k) programs are a good vehicle because many companies provide corporate matching. Or if you don't have access to a 401(k), an IRA account gives even more flexibility in the range of possible investments.

  Some firms, big and small, are freezing pension plans or scaling back or cutting off their matching contributions to 401(k) plans. It's important that you *not* follow suit. Try to stick with your savings plan and perhaps even boost your contribution.

  Note that in the previous recession (2000–2002), the average 401(k) balance of workers who continued to contribute fell just 8 percent, according to the Employee Benefits Research Institute (EBRI). And that compares to the S&P 500's plunge of 47 percent. Not only did ongoing contributions soften the blow of market losses, but a year later, the average 401(k) balance of those savers was up 30 percent.

  Also, you may have gotten out of the habit of looking at your account statements. But I'd urge you to review them and make sure your holdings are diversified. Ignoring your savings, or discontinuing them, will come back to bite you someday.

- **Build up your emergency fund.** Cash is always welcome. And with joblessness still rising and access to home-equity lines of credit being reduced, you owe it to yourself to be prepared for anything. Four to six months of expenses socked away in a savings account or money-market account should get you through the tight spots.

- **Stash your pennies from heaven.** Get in the habit of not spending windfalls, however small. Any nonrecurring sums—bonuses, inheritances, tax refunds, medical insurance reimbursements, money from the second job . . . you name it—can be socked away for retirement. Because this money isn't part of your regular income, it's a fairly painless way to save.

  Similarly, if you're paid biweekly, that means you have two months a year when you receive three paychecks. Put some or all of that extra paycheck away for retirement.

  And you if get a raise, bank it.

- **Guard against inflation.** Though the Federal Reserve suggests inflation won't become a problem anytime soon, many others think inflation could come roaring back to life because the federal government has been spending money like a drunken sailor. (Actually, that's probably a libel on drunken sailors. It's doubtful they spend that wantonly.) So, as we'll see in later chapters, it may be smart to have a portion of your fixed-income investments in Treasury inflation-protected securities, or TIPS. These bonds are backed by the U.S. government, like normal Treasuries, but also have built-in protections that boost returns when inflation rages.

Spending Less

Those are steps you might take to put away more. But, of course, spending less is also a key to saving. So here are some ideas for that side of the ledger:

- **Raise your deductibles.** Premiums for employer-sponsored health insurance rose to $13,375 annually for family coverage in 2009, according to the Kaiser Family Foundation, with employees on average paying $3,515. What's more, other statistics suggest $1,954 is spent on car insurance and $804 on a homeowner's policy. All told, that's more than $520 per month on insurance premiums alone. Smart spenders can sidestep some of that cost by raising their deductibles.

They can also explore health-savings accounts and check life-insurance costs as well.

In fact, Consumerreports.org says raising your homeowners' insurance deductible from $250 to $1,000 can save you 25 percent. It's worth looking into. Similarly, take advantage of discounts, such as combining multiple policies at one insurer.

- **Weatherize**. Your retirement fund could be leaking out your doors and windows. According to the Energy Information Administration, which is the federal government's source of energy statistics, the average household spends $1,137 each winter in heating alone. Because it's said that consumers save 3 percent of their heating bill for every degree they turn down their thermostat, lowering that thermostat just 5 percent would reduce heating costs by 15 percent. Even more may come by making sure your windows and doors are weather-stripped and that you've got timers installed on heating and air-conditioning systems. (Maybe there'll even be some future tax credit available, something along the lines of "Cash for Caulking.")
- **Choose your vacations wisely.** A study by Visa found that the average consumer plans to spend $1,654 per person on a summer vacation. But if you're diligent about scouting hot vacation deals and going in the off-season, you can save a bundle on hotels and airfare.
- **Use less gasoline.** According to the Renewable Fuels Association, the average gasoline consumption per household is 1,052 gallons per year, or about 88 gallons a month. At $3 a gallon, that's almost $300 a month, and probably a big chunk of your monthly budget. Public transportation, car pooling, walking, biking, and the like probably would be good for your health as well as your wealth.
- **Find cheap or free entertainment.** Cultural events are great, but consumers can just as easily opt for free or low-cost concerts, lectures, outdoor movies, and art shows. Even doing that one night per weekend can easily reduce your entertainment costs by, say, $100 a month, or $1,200 a year. Getting books, movies, CDs, and other entertainment from the library could further bolster that. Do you really watch those premium cable-TV channels enough to justify the cost? Do you really need to eat out as often as you do?

- **Bargain shop.** The Internet is great for scoping out bargains, whether for plane tickets, hotels, or rental cars. Sites like Craigslist.com, Priceline.com, Overstock.com, and Restaurants .com, etc. are super for finding all manner of used goods or discounts. And, of course, many alternatives—such as Vonage or Skype—have sprung up for cutting the phone bill. Similarly, you can easily shop around for deals on lots of other online purchases.

Rethink Your Retirement Years

People's ideas about retirement have taken their lumps in the past couple of years. Yes, diversification helped. But most of us have lost a lot of money since the market peaked in 2007. (The typical bond fund lost about 30 percent less than the typical stock fund. Nonetheless, many more asset classes were crushed simultaneously than is normally the case.) And all of us have lost a lot of time. So what to do?

Well, for starters, don't give up and, as I said, don't beat yourself up. The world is not coming to an end. Sure, your investments likely got mauled as the S&P 500 lost 37 percent of its value in 2008. And the market was "unfair" to do that. After all, you did the right things: worked hard, contributed to your 401(k), sought to diversify your investments. But maybe you still feel kind of stupid.

Feelings, though, aren't facts. You still have time to do the smart thing—and it may not be as difficult as you think to get back on track.

For instance, for investors within five years of retiring, adding just one or two more years on the job can put them on pace for retirement, according to a study of 401(k) and other defined-contribution plans. Financial Engines, an investment advisory firm, said that while most people assume big losses will take many years from which to recover, that's not always the case. It points to the fact that retirement income from Social Security and future savings is not affected by the recent decline. For savers who began 2008 on track to replace 70 percent of their income in retirement in a few years, portfolio declines of 23 percent to 30 percent mean only a 10 percent to 19 percent decrease in projected median retirement income.

So, assuming you can hold onto your job in this economy, working one or two extra years will solve the problem in some situations, according to the study. The researchers noted that working longer doesn't mean recouping all your losses but rather getting to a place where retirement is possible.

The cost of the market decline in 2008, while severe, in many cases is more modest than it first appears. That's because delaying retirement means setting aside more money, plus letting your savings grow for a longer time. What's more, delaying Social Security benefits means a higher monthly payout. While there's no simple rule of thumb that applies to everybody, there are reasonable actions that, if taken, can help people get back on track.

So let's look in more detail at what might be done:

- **Calmly assess your situation.** *First, weigh your current employment.* If you have a job, how secure do you feel? How marketable are you if you lose the job? If you're underemployed or unemployed, how long can you support yourself on current resources, or will you need to dip into retirement resources?

  Next, ask: "How healthy am I?" Your expected longevity will color your decisions. We all hope to live to an old age, but a longer life brings with it the risk of outliving your savings and income. The average life expectancy today of someone 65 years old is more than 85. So, with life expectancies on the rise, it's probably best to assume you'll live longer than you expect.

  Then, examine your expenses. Look in detail at what you spend. I mentioned in the previous section some of the likely targets—entertainment and dining, insurance deductibles, cable, cell phone, and the like.

  Fourth, get a handle on how much you really need to save for retirement. About half of Americans (44 percent) have calculated the number but roughly an equal proportion have simply guessed at it, according to the EBRI survey.

  Fifth, what assets will you have to draw upon? In addition to your retirement accounts and personal savings, do you own lifetime-income annuities or other investments? Will you be eligible for a traditional pension? Does it include a cost-of-living adjustment? Will your spouse continue to receive it after you die? Have you gotten an estimate of the monthly benefits from your human-resources department as well as an estimate of your Social Security benefits? Is an inheritance likely or possible?

Sixth, consider getting a good financial advisor to assist you. She can give you a hand on refining your retirement savings target and suggest strategies for getting there—preferably a *Buckets of Money* strategy from a *Buckets of Money* specialist.

- **Check your timeline.** Figuring out how to deal with retirement issues depends on where you are in your life. Time is perhaps the most important element in building—or rebuilding—a portfolio. So it's important to break this down into age groupings:

Under 40. This is the luckiest group. Two things are working in its favor. The market will eventually recover and grow. And, by saving early and regularly, these young investors can get the benefit of compounding, meaning early savings will build upon themselves. So, given their long-term outlook, the recent drop in share prices is an opportunity for them.

In fact, a new study by T. Rowe Price shows that young investors who began systematically buying equities in past severe bear markets *were significantly better off 30 years hence than investors who began in bull markets.* That's because they could buy more shares more cheaply at the beginning. By making systematic investment and reinvesting dividends, they then put themselves in a better position to gain from future bull markets.

From 40 to 55. You're likely at the height of your earning power, so this is a time to invest as much as you can in your 401(k) while also seeking other ways to sock away money. You may want to take advantage of "catch-up" contributions that allow workers 50 and older to kick in an extra $5,500 annually in 401(k) contributions or $1,000 extra each year in IRA contributions.

Fifty-five and over. What's important to this group is to recognize where you are right now and try not to think about where you were in 2007. If you're already in or near retirement, you're probably going to need to work longer, save more, and/or spend less.

Again, consider the possibility of catch-up contributions to your 401(k) or IRA. You may be tempted to retreat to a conservative stance, but the wisdom of that move is debatable.

If you're already retired, check with your financial advisor about withdrawing less money than you originally planned until the economy rebounds. A common guideline recommends withdrawing 4 percent of your savings in the first year of retirement, then bumping up your withdrawal by about 3 percent each subsequent year to keep pace with inflation. But in a down market, maybe you'd be better off to skip those annual increases or revert to your 4 percent withdrawal of your new, reduced balance.

- **Don't raid your retirement accounts early.** Do whatever you can to avoid this scenario. You'll lose the benefits of compounding *and* could lose as much as 40 percent of your distribution to taxes and penalties. More on this later in this chapter.
- **Plan to work longer.** One of the really important things for anybody who is retired or about to retire is to recognize that the picture is changing. Your retirement may not resemble your parents' retirement. Many people are going to need to work a little longer or find a way to earn a bit of money in retirement.

According to the new EBRI Retirement Confidence Survey, 28 percent of workers expect to work longer because of the economic downturn, with 9 out of 10 figuring to postpone retirement as a way of increasing their financial security.

The percentage of people planning to retire later—at age 66 or after—jumped from 9 percent in 1998 to 31 percent in 2009, according to EBRI. An ongoing survey by MetLife Mature Market Institute found that only 15 percent of those who said they would retire in 2008 actually did so. And an analysis by T. Rowe Price showed that someone who worked an additional three years beyond age 62, saved 25 percent of his or her gross income, and delayed collecting Social Security benefits until age 66 would increase total retirement income by 28 percent.

But, understand, things don't always work out that way. According to EBRI, the median worker expects to retire at age 65, with roughly one in five planning to stay on the job into their 70s. But, the median retired person stopped actually working at age 62. Nearly half of those retirees stopped working *sooner* than they planned.

Whether for reasons of their own health or the health of a family member forcing a change, or just being downsized out of a job, working longer is not as discretionary as we sometimes view it. So if working longer is your plan—and your *only* plan—you could run into problems because needing to work longer doesn't mean you'll be able to.

If you can manage it, though, delaying retirement does five things: (1) increases current income; (2) avoids the reduction in Social Security benefits; (3) allows you to contribute more to a 401(k) plan; (4) allows that plan to accumulate more investment income; and (5) shortens the period of retirement, thus reducing the amount of money you'll need (or upping the quality of your retirement lifestyle). And, of course, a few extra years on the job could mean continued access to employer-provided health insurance.

- **Plan on possible part-time work in retirement.** Maybe you need to scale back your optimal retirement scenario. Instead of having all that time to play bridge or buff that '57 Chevy in the garage, maybe you'll need to work two or three days a week. Perhaps you can even serve as a consultant to your present employer or at another company. Or take a part-time role somewhere else. There are worse outcomes, especially if you can work at something that at least mildly interests you. Building income beats tapping other resources. And the payoff could be significant. For example, if you spend 5 percent of your assets each year in retirement and you could make just $20,000 working, that would be the equivalent of having $400,000 of investment assets spinning off cash for you.

- **Play head-ups with Social Security.** There's more to Social Security than just paying in for decades and decades and hoping you'll get something back. In fact, it's helpful to think of your Social Security as an asset that you can do a certain amount of strategizing with. Take today's maximum monthly benefit of $2,235 at full retirement age. To generate that much income for life, you'd need the equivalent of a $550,000 nest egg. So maybe that's something worth spending a little time to figure out.

Normal retirement age for receiving full benefits is now 66. Of course, you can start as early age 62—and that's what most people do—but your benefits will be reduced by

25 percent or more. Plus, there's a financial penalty for working if you start benefits before your normal retirement age. By contrast, for every year you wait up until age 70, your benefits will go up by about 8 percent a year in addition to an annual cost-of-living benefit. And, of course, not all of your Social Security earnings are taxable; that percentage depends on your total income.

A number of strategies exist that allow you to make the most of your Social Security. For instance, a spouse in some cases can defer his or her own benefits and take half of the other spouse's benefits until reaching age 70. At that point he or she can file for his/her own full benefits (which have been growing at 8 percent annually) and give up the spousal benefits.

Or, did you begin benefits at age 62 but have come to regret the smaller payout? You can choose to pay the Social Security Administration back all the benefits you've received, withdraw your early-retirement application and then reapply for full benefits at age 66 or later. You'd need to have a lot of cash to do that, but, on the other hand, you'd eventually get quite a boost in benefits, not to mention having had, in effect, an interest-free and penalty-free loan from Social Security for all those years.

The point is that your Social Security benefits aren't just a lump that must be passively accepted. There's some flexibility there. Of course, some of these strategies come with tax and other financial considerations. So it's a good idea to talk to a competent advisor before making any moves.

- **Ponder lifestyle changes.** Depending on your level of interest and/or desperation, you could take more radical steps to help jump-start your retirement plans. You could, for instance, downsize your home. If you're willing to sell and move to a less expensive home, you can plow the profit into your retirement account. You probably won't owe taxes on the first $500,000 in capital gains if you're married and have lived in the home for two years or more. In addition, you'll probably have lower property taxes on the new place and perhaps less maintenance. Or you could move to a less expensive part of the country. Leaving family and friends is a big tradeoff, but it may be worth considering. However, be sure to take into account how the taxes would be in the new state.

- **Take care of you first.** Sure, it'd be nice to see your kids leave college debt-free as well as maybe inherit a bunch of money when you die. But, remember, they can borrow to get their education, but generally you can't borrow your way through retirement. Similarly, lightening up on your presumed legacy might help ensure a comfortable retirement. And if you explain your options, the kiddos will likely understand.

- **Give some thought to a reverse mortgage.** If you're sitting on a huge chunk of equity in your house—a home you like and don't want to sell—and are over age 62, a reverse mortgage could yield a lump sum of cash, a line or credit, or a predetermined monthly amount. The loan comes due when you move or die. Of course, this reduces your home equity, which may be one of your biggest assets. In addition, you'd want to investigate the high closing costs and think about how long you plan on keeping the house. But if you're a retiree facing a serious lack of income, reducing your equity may be preferable to reducing your standard of living.

  On the other hand, if your kids are doing well, you might want to work out a de facto reverse mortgage with them. If they're going to inherit your home anyway, perhaps they'd be open to the idea of helping you out with, say, $1,000 a month from their own home-equity line of credit. In effect, they become the reverse-mortgage lender—but without most of the fees. They can deduct the interest they pay on their home-equity loan, subject to certain limits and the Alternative Minimum Tax (AMT). And after your death, they inherit the house free of any capital gains tax. It might be worth discussing.

Retool Your Retirement Savings Plans

As mentioned, it's important that you not let economic jitters change your savings habits. Stick with the tried-and-true practice of socking away as much as possible in your 401(k) or IRA, or both.

In some cases, employers have stopped contributing to 401(k)s. But if you do likewise, several things—*all bad*—will happen: (1) you'll miss out on a valuable tax deduction. For instance, if you contribute $4,000 to your 401(k) and you're in the 25 percent federal tax bracket, you'll save $1,000 in federal income taxes, plus possible state tax savings; (2) you'll miss out on the compounding of that contribution over time; and (3) you'll miss out on the chance to pick up further stock-market bargains in your retirement account.

Other retirement-savings gambits to consider:

- **See if you or your spouse is eligible for an IRA.** If you can, of course, you should consider putting away the maximum in a 401(k)-type plan. But also check to see if you or your spouse can contribute to either a deductible or a Roth IRA. Income limits apply, but depending on your tax bracket, one or the other will most certainly make sense. Even if one of you is covered by an employer-sponsored plan, such as a 401(k), there's a chance the uncovered spouse could fund a deductible IRA, again depending on your income. The general rule of thumb: If you're in the 15 percent marginal-income tax bracket, fund the Roth; in the 25 percent or greater bracket, fund a deductible plan.

- **Switch to a Roth IRA to offset losses.** If you have an IRA, the balance is likely a lot smaller than it was a year or two ago. Thus, this could be a good time to convert your traditional IRA to a Roth IRA. You must pay taxes on the entire amount you convert, but the lower your account value, the smaller your tax bill. And you can convert as much or as little as you like.

  The Roth is a marvelous retirement-savings mechanism. Although you can't take a tax deduction for contributions—as you can with a traditional IRA or 401(k) or similar employer-based retirement fund—all your earnings grow tax-deferred. Then, once you turn age 59½ and the account has been open at least five years, all your withdrawals are tax-free. By contrast, withdrawals from traditional IRAs and 401(k) plans are taxed at your ordinary income-tax rate.

  No one knows what future tax laws will be. But with big budget deficits comes the widespread fear that tax rates will rise to pay for burgeoning government spending. Thus, future tax-free income becomes especially alluring. In short, by paying lower taxes today you may be able to avoid what could be higher taxes tomorrow. However, this certainly is not the case for everyone. So some good tax planning and forecasting is in order before you act.

The year 2010 is especially critical for those considering this strategy. Income limits on Roth IRA conversions disappear in 2010, meaning anyone will be able to convert retirement assets to a Roth starting that year. What's more, if you do so in 2010, you can spread your tax bill over two years. You won't need to pay the first installment until 2012, when you file your 2011 tax return, and you can pay the balance when you file your 2012 return in 2013.

While the elimination of the income-eligibility limits on Roth *conversions* is permanent, the chance to spread the tax bill over two years is a one-time-only opportunity. Income limits on Roth IRA *contributions*, however, will remain in effect, so be sure to talk to your financial advisor about those.

- **Tapping early—and reluctantly—into your retirement savings.** Most 401(k) and similar employer-based plans allow you to borrow up to half of your account balance (to a limit of 50 percent of your balance, or $50,000, whichever is less) and repay the loan over five years. But, of course, that can take a huge bite out of your future savings because you lose the power of compounding.

What's more, if you change or lose your job, the loan may come due immediately. And if you fail to repay the loan, the money you got will be treated as a distribution subject to state and federal income taxes, plus a 10 percent early-withdrawal federal-tax penalty (and maybe even a state-tax penalty) if you're under age 59½. Some plans offer hardship withdrawals that don't need to be repaid. But those are still subject to taxes and penalties.

You can't borrow from a traditional IRA, but you can withdraw your money at any time, provided you pay taxes on the withdrawal. If you're younger than 59½, you'll pay a 10 percent federal penalty and possibly a state one, too. With a Roth IRA, you can withdraw your contributions (but not the earnings) at any time tax-free and penalty-free.

But, as should be clear by now, you should try to avoid early withdrawals unless you're facing a severe financial emergency. Money taken out will stunt the growth of your retirement savings.

Reinvent Your Strategy

And now we get to the nub: What should be your new, overall strategy for retiring in comfort and safety? How can you take advantage of the growth potential of stocks and real estate without subjecting yourself to the market's stomach-churning volatility?

Well, for starters, let me explain that I believe the entire financial services industry has been doing retirement planning wrong. They create beautiful, colorful pie charts representing some asset-allocation model. Then they take a systematic, pro rata withdrawal to support one's retirement income, and then rebalance the accounts to remain consistent with your predetermined asset-allocation model. Practically every financial advisor, mutual fund company, and online planner does it that way.

Voicing doubt about the wisdom of that flawed concept is, of course, heresy and not at all what you hear from pundits and financial journalists. But it's one thing to write or pontificate about retirement; it's another thing to be responsible for people's livelihoods as I have for more than 30 years, taking my fair share of lumps along the way. Understand, I view the whole subject of retirement and retirement planning very seriously. If a journalist or pundit screws up and makes a bad recommendation, he moves on or, at worst, writes or voices a retraction. But if a financial advisor screws up, his client may end up eating dog food at retirement. That's why when people's financial lives and retirement years depend on you and you are their trusted financial advisor, you better know your stuff because you never know when your clients will be faced with a 1966, 1973, 2000, or 2008 when their net worth shrinks before their very eyes. It's impossible to predict the next financial crisis, recession, depression, terrorist act, tsunami, or earthquake. That's why you need a bullet-proof plan. And that's why I created the *Buckets of Money* strategy that's now been used successfully by thousands of individuals nationwide.

Income and Growth

You want to invest soundly, conservatively. You don't want to bet the farm on the short-term gyrations of an erratic stock market. But neither do you wish to invest so timidly that inflation erodes your nest egg. So how can you do both: receive income *and* get the growth that stocks and other long-term investments can bring?

That's where the three buckets come into play. Think of them as short-term (Bucket 1, "Income"), mid-term (Bucket 2, "Relative Safety"), and long-term (Bucket 3, "Growth"). While there are subcategories as well, it may be simplest to think of the buckets as Income, Safety, and Growth, or short-term, mid-term, and long-term. You'll want to split your money, putting some into each bucket.

How you divide the money will depend on (a) how much you have to invest, (b) how much income you will need to live on and when you need it, (c) how many years you need that income for, and (d) what rate of return and rate of inflation you predict.

Academic Corroboration

In June 2007 I took great interest in an article in the *Journal of Financial Planning* called "Is Rebalancing Your Portfolio During Retirement Necessary?" Written by two State University of New York professors, John Spitzer, Ph.D., and Sandeep Singh, CFA, Ph.D., it recounted their extensive study of which retirement-distribution strategies worked best and which assets to tap into first in order to fund a sustainable inflation-adjusted retirement income. Their conclusion confirmed what I have been saying and doing for more than 18 years: Spending down a safe bucket (such as Treasuries, CDs, and bonds) first, while leaving a riskier bucket (real estate and stocks) to grow before tapping it produced the *best* results . . . let me repeat, the *best* results.

To quote the professors' executive summary: "Withdrawing bonds first, over stocks, performs the best of all methods. . . ." Notice they didn't say second best or third best but rather *the* best! And, they continued: "This method also is most apt to leave a larger remaining balance at the end of 30 years, while rebalancing leaves the smallest amount."

This distribution methodology represents an oversimplified version of my *Buckets of Money* strategy. The strategy of spending down bonds or fixed investments first (Buckets 1 and 2) and stocks and real estate last (Bucket 3) was scientifically proven, based on solid academic research, to produce the best results. The so-called rebalancing method—the pie chart allocation with systematic withdrawals used most frequently by mutual fund companies, financial planners, and brokers—has now been proven to produce the worst results.

So why does Wall Street and the financial-planning community gravitate toward the asset-allocation, rebalancing method? The answer is actually quite simple. The rebalancing method is the most popular choice because it's simple, profitable for the firm, and easy to implement. It enables the sales people and investment firms to maximize their fee income. It's easy to charge a wrap fee on 100 percent of a client's assets, be they stocks, bonds, or cash. By contrast, with a *Buckets of Money* strategy, the fees charged may only be on 30 percent to 40 percent of the total assets, thus a firm would lose 60 percent to 70 percent in fees. (Depending on the product, some advisors may receive upfront commissions. But those are usually priced into the product and not paid directly by the investor.)

But it's not just about the fees. Most brokerage platforms can't give you a consolidated report if multiple asset classes are used, especially if they're not sold by the firm. Furthermore, a nice, pretty report helps justify the advisors' existence, whether they are adding value or not.

I know how the Wall Street model works because I've attended most of the same classes your advisor has, and I train advisors all across the country. So I have a good idea of what's presented, and the scenario goes like this: The investor, advisor, or fund company simply creates an asset-allocation model including large and small stocks, growth and value stocks along with bonds, invested domestically and internationally. And when it comes time for a distribution, they send you 4 percent to 5 percent annually by taking a systematic withdrawal, pro rata, from each of the accounts. Then at regular intervals (monthly, quarterly, or annually), the accounts are rebalanced to reflect the original asset allocation. This technique may be acceptable during your accumulation phase (although I still favor a Buckets approach), but when it comes to distributing your income stream, it's decidedly inferior and significantly more costly over the long term.

A Final Word

To rebound from the recent financial meltdown, you probably need to rebuild your savings, rethink your retirement years, and retool your retirement savings plans. The first involves, of course, saving more and spending less, while the second entails calmly assessing your situation and deciding, for instance, whether you need to work longer or work part-time after you retire.

You also need to give some thought to making the most of your retirement savings plans—such as IRAs and 401(k)s. And, most of all, it's essential to come up with a strategy for retiring in comfort and safety. That's where the *Buckets of Money* plan comes into play. In the past, some pundits have been critical of my concept of spending down the "safe" money in Bucket 1 while allowing the other buckets to grow over time. But it's clear now that they were wrong, and academic research has vindicated me. In short, *Buckets of Money* works, and it's cheaper for you.

So let's look in more detail at how—and why—it works.

PART

II

FORGE A NEW PLAN

CHAPTER

3

Grasp the Buckets of Money Concept

Successful investing is as much about *time* as it is about picking the right securities. So if you can "buy" time by having a reliable source of steady income in retirement while you allow your stocks and real estate to grow for 15 years or more, you have a statistical assurance that you're going to make money. (That's not the same as a guarantee, but it's about as close as a mortal can hope for.)

Stripped to its simplest, that's the premise of the *Buckets of Money* plan: You organize your investments into three main groupings, or "buckets"—and take almost all the risk in Bucket 3 with stocks and real estate. And then—other than possibly taking some dividends from the growth-and-income category of Bucket 3—*you don't touch* that bucket. While there are many possible variations, the basic strategy is just this: You live by spending down the first two, relatively "safe" buckets while time mitigates those risks in Bucket 3.

If you're like most retirees or preretirees, you hunger for stability, yet yearn for growth to rejuvenate your portfolio that was battered the past couple years. *Buckets of Money* offers a reassuring—and scientifically proven—strategy that gives investors both growth *and* income. Thus, this strategy can shield you from the short-term ups and downs of the market. It'll give you the courage and discipline to stay invested no matter what the future holds. It'll help you plan your retirement years with greater confidence.

In this chapter we'll dig into the science of this—that is, the science of money, not the art of speculation—and why this system works. And in Chapter 4, we'll get into specifics of what you could put in your buckets as well as some detailed examples showing how that could work for you. And in later chapters, you'll be given refinements, such as how annuities, home equity, REITs, and taxes figure into this picture. And, finally, you'll be shown how to withdraw money in retirement as well as how to ensure that enjoyment, not just money, is your primary focus.

Put Time on Your Side

Remember how Jim Croce sang "If I could put time in a bottle . . ."? Well, of course, we can't. But as investors we can do the next best thing: We can put time on our side. We do that by investing in stocks and having the discipline not to jump in and out of the market. Somebody once said that the stock market is a mechanism for transferring money from the impatient to the patient. It's that impatience—that repeatedly buying high, then panicking and selling low—that keeps the average investor from doing even as well as the average mutual fund or matching the market averages.

And it is times like this—following a big correction—that offer the prospect of outsized gains. Take the 1929 crash, for example. If you'd invested $500,000 one day in 1929, you would've awakened a couple years later with—what?—maybe $200,000.

Of course, you would've been shocked to see what was happening to your portfolio, especially if you were drawing income from it to live on. So what do you think you would've done? Well, you might have freaked out, sworn off stocks, and moved 100 percent of your money to cash. If so and if you were taking out 4 percent a year of your original $500,000 adjusted for deflation (yes, back then we had deflation, not inflation) for living expenses . . . you'd be broke by 1946 because your cash wasn't growing as fast as you were taking it out.

If in 1932—four years after the cataclysmic decline—you had allocated 25 percent of your $200,000 to stocks, you wouldn't have gone broke until 1950. If you'd left 50 percent in the stock market, you would've survived until 1957. And if you'd kept 75 percent of your money in stocks and continued to take out that 4 percent each year, you would've had $1.7 million by 1992.

What's more, if you'd thrown caution to the wind and you'd left 100 percent of your money in the stock market (probably not advisable), by 1992 you would've had $42 million!

The point is, you must be in the market to enjoy the benefits of the market. And even during dismal times like the present, it's good to remember that we have recovered from dismal times in the past.

The risk of losing money in stocks is quite significant *over short time periods*. If you invest for one year, you have about a 72 percent chance of making money and, thus, a 28 percent chance of losing money. But if you can invest in stocks and leave your money alone for, say, five years, you've got about an 87 percent chance of making money. And here's the kicker: If you buy stocks and don't touch your stock market money for 15 years, you are statistically assured of making money. That's because in all of history there's never been a 15-year period in which stocks have lost money.

So that's what I mean about buying time. And the *Buckets of Money* plan is based on setting up your accounts so that you can leave your stock-market (and real estate) money untouched.

Other Risks

But the up and downs of the stock market risk is only one risk you face. Lots of other risks exist that you need to manage if you're going to be a successful investor. For instance, there's interest rate risk. Rates are quite low now. And when they go up—and they will at some point—bonds will go down in value. So that makes positioning your portfolio critical. The *Buckets of Money* strategy will help you navigate that risk, too.

Inflation risk is another obstacle. With the trillions and trillions of dollars the government is spending to stimulate the economy come the risk of debasing the dollar. That means, the value of the dollar goes down, and it takes a lot more dollars to buy the same amount of goods and services.

As you can see in Figure 3.1, the only real investments that are going to make you money over the long haul are stocks and/or real estate. So while you do need to have safe money in bonds and cash, you need a commitment to the stock market, as tough as that may be to stomach after having gone through what we've all just gone through.

Stocks, Bonds, Bills, and Inflation 1926–2008

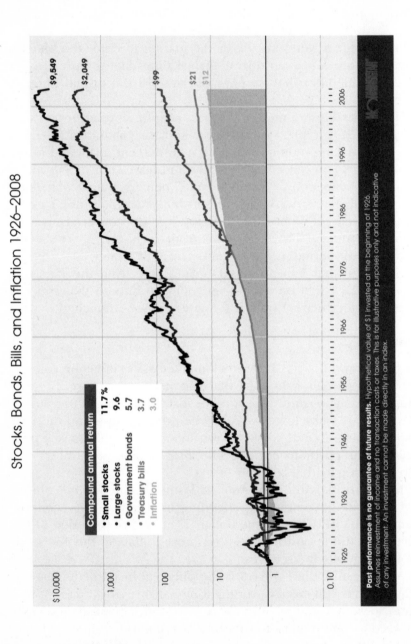

Compound annual return	
• Small stocks	11.7%
• Large stocks	9.6
• Government bonds	5.7
• Treasury bills	3.7
• Inflation	3.0

$9,549

$2,049

$99

$21
$12

Past performance is no guarantee of future results. Hypothetical value of $1 invested at the beginning of 1926. Assumes reinvestment of income and no transaction costs or taxes. This is for illustrative purposes only and not indicative of any investment. An investment cannot be made directly in an index.

Figure 3.1 Returns Before and After Inflation

Source:

Performance of Dow Jones Industrial Average after a Major Crisis

Event	First Trading Day After Crisis	1 Year Later	2 Years Later
Berlin Blockade	June 25, 1948	−6.2%	31.7%
Korean War	June 26, 1950	21.1%	40.7%
Cuban Missile Crisis	October 23, 1962	38.8%	70.1%
Kennedy Assassination	November 22, 1963	30.2%	44.8%
Gulf of Tonkin	August 5, 1964	10.8%	12.7%
OPEC Oil Embargo	October 18, 1973	−26.8%	−3.3%
Iran Hostage/Oil Crisis	November 5, 1979	22.3%	16.3%
Persian Gulf War	August 3, 1990	10.0%	27.5%
Russian Bond Default	September 3, 1998	47.2%	53.8%
Average		*16.4%*	*32.7%*

Figure 3.2   Doomsday It Isn't
Source: Dreman Value Management, LLC.

Then there's event risk. You remember how the market plunged after 9/11? Well, it did the same during the Berlin blockade, the Korean War, the Cuban missile crisis, and any number of other then-seemingly catastrophic events.

If you look at Figure 3.2, you'll see how, on average, the stock market rebounded two years later by about 32 percent. So remember when I said you have to be in the market to enjoy the benefits of the market? Well, sometimes you need to be in the market even during the dark times. If we've now hit bottom, or are near the bottom, chances are from this point forward, your return in stocks could be excellent. But even if they aren't excellent next year or the year after, chances are that 15 to 25 years from now when we'll need to get our hands on the stock bucket, the likelihood is that stocks will have produced a return that exceeds all other asset classes.

Another risk that we don't like to think about is longevity risk: outliving our money. The Society of Actuaries tells us that with a healthy married couple aged 65, there's about a 52 percent chance one or the other will make it to age 92 and more than a 25 percent chance one or the other will get all the way to age 97. Wow! That's great, but that's also scary because it means you need to design your portfolio so you don't run out of money before you run out of time. A *Buckets of Money* strategy can help you do that, too.

Wall Street's Answer

The *Buckets of Money* idea of putting a chunk of your money in stocks and real estate and leaving it there untouched for years isn't an idea that's taking Wall Street by storm. Why? Most of Wall Street—including big brokerages and discount firms—make their money trading. You don't earn a lot in the way of fees unless you trade a lot. If you believe the Wall Streeters (and I include here the TV pundits and magazine and newsletter writers who echo the Street's party line), the way to get rich is to be nimble: jump in and out of the market at the right times.

But you'd need to be very, *very* nimble . . . and there's no evidence anybody has ever been able to do that consistently. Meanwhile, Wall Street's still getting paid.

For instance, as shown in Figure 3.3, if you'd put a dollar in the stock market in 1926 and then left it alone, you would've had $2,049 by the end of 2008. But if you'd missed the 34 best months, you would've had $20.25.

So which months should you be in and which should you be out? Can anyone actually figure that out in advance? I don't think so, and many studies back me up.

Researchers at Duke University, for example, studied market-timing newsletters over a 12-year period and "found strong evidence that as a group, newsletters cannot time the market." In fact, in one study only 11 of 237 newsletter strategies "could be deemed superior in the long run," researchers said. "This number is fewer than one would expect by pure chance." And *Hulbert Financial Digest*, a respected source of newsletter information, studied market timers for a 10-year period found that the S&P 500 gained 18 percent but none of the market timers equaled that and the average newsletter got only a 10 percent return.

Further, numerous financial journal articles and studies from universities all around the nation have come to the same conclusion: You just can't do it.

Another study by SEI (see Table 3.1) showed what happens when the market turns around after a sharp correction. If you reinvest at the very bottom, you'll earn 32.5 percent in that first year and your portfolio could recover its full value in 1.5 years. But if you're a week late, your return drops to 24.3 percent, and your recovery time grows to 2.5 years. And being a quarter late drops your return to 14.8 percent and lengthens the recovery time to three years.

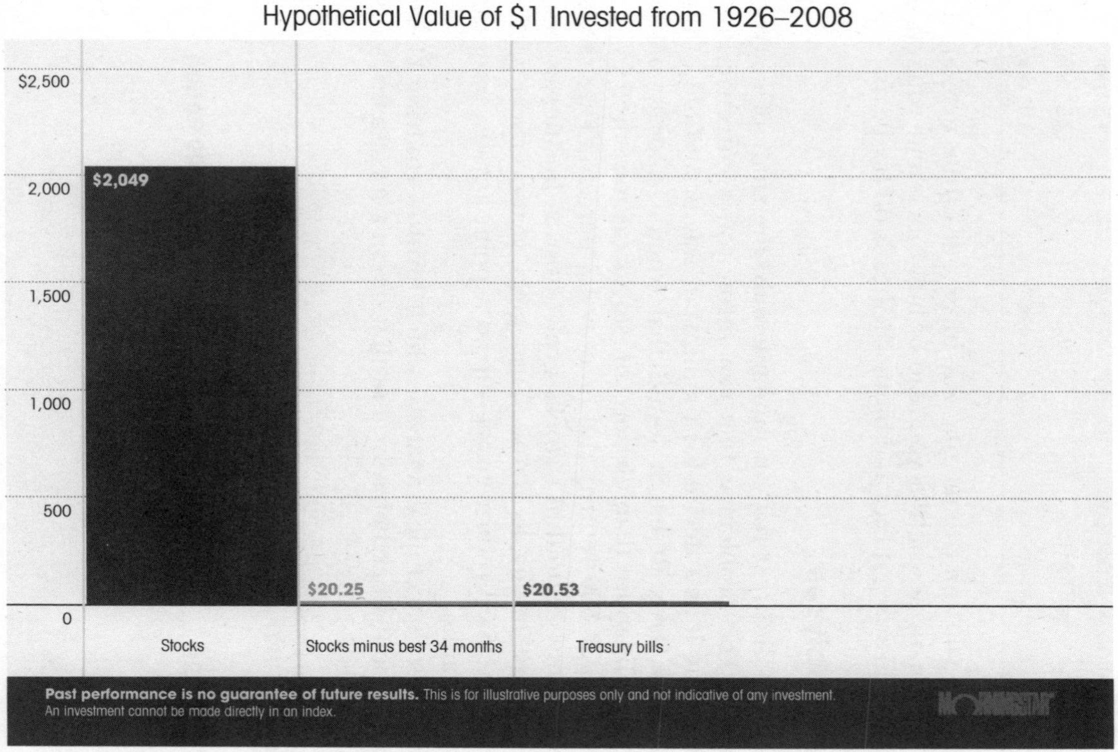
Hypothetical Value of $1 Invested from 1926–2008
$2,500
2,000
1,500
1,000
500
0
$2,049
$20.25
$20.53
Stocks
Stocks minus best 34 months
Treasury bills
Past performance is no guarantee of future results. This is for illustrative purposes only and not indicative of any investment.
An investment cannot be made directly in an index.

Figure 3.3 Dangers of Market Timing

Source: © 2009 Morningstar, Inc. All rights reserved.

Table 3.1   Market Timing Doesn't Work

Investors Who:	Gains After 1 Year	Broke Even After
Rode the market down & back up	32.50%	1.5 Years
Jumped back in 1 week too late	24.30%	2.5 Years
Jumped back in 3 months too late	14.80%	3.0 Years

In short, you can't time your way in or out of the market, no matter how many newsletters you read or how much time you watch TV pundits throwing things and biting the heads off toy bears.

Flawed Analyses

Others on Wall Street rely on fundamentals: the study of markets and profits. The problem is that can throw you a curveball, too, if you're using it as a device for timing your way in and out of the market. Ned Davis Research found that when corporate profits are growing by more than 20 percent, stocks (as measured by the annualized S&P 500 return) rise by only 1.3 percent. That seems counterintuitive. Shouldn't stocks grow most as businesses post greater profits? In fact, as Figure 3.4 suggests, year-over-year profits decline as the S&P return grows—up to a point anyway, until the market also tanks.

Then there's technical analysis, which involves studying charts for signals about stock behavior. But that doesn't consistently work

Year-Over-Year Earnings Growth
from March 31, 1927, to September 30, 2003

Profit Change	Annualized S&P 500 Return
• Above 20%	1.3%
• 20% to 10%	5.8%
• 10% to −10%	9.3%
• −10% to −25%	28.6%
• −25% and below	−28.2%

Figure 3.4   Wall Street Says Use Fundamental Analysis
Source: Ned Davis Research, *USA Today*, Monday October 27, 2003.

either. Burton Malkiel, a Princeton professor and author of the classic *A Random Walk Down Wall Street*, studied 548 stocks traded on the New York Stock Exchange over a five-year period and found no relationship between the technical signal and the subsequent performance. Following the signals left you no better than if you bought and held. In fact, the best strategy was to *buy after a sell signal!* So much for that reading of the tea leaves.

Researchers on Wall Street and in academia are pretty much unanimous in saying nobody can really figure out how to time the market . . . or match profits and losses to stock prices . . . or decipher the arcane language of charts. So is some TV talking head or broker going to be able to foretell what the future holds for stocks? I don't think so.

If they could, they and their clients would be billionaires, but most are not. In fact, you can check on many of the "top" money gurus at cxoAdvisory.com, which grades the prognosticators. The last time I checked, they were right only about 46 percent of the time. Got a coin? Flip it, and you're right 50 percent of the time. *Ha!* You, too, can be a guru.

Main Street's Myopia

Nor can you rely on mainstream prognosticators, like the money magazines. Sure, they all ballyhoo their picks for the "10 Great Stocks to Own *Now!*" or "Can't-Go-Wrong Mutual Funds!" But almost invariably they're chasing the best performers. And the best performers one year rarely are the best the following year.

It's human nature, I suppose, to chase the best performers. We look at a stock that's soaring, and we say, "I got to get some of that. It's going to the moon." And, indeed, some stocks really do skyrocket. But you know what happens to skyrockets? They eventually plummet back to earth.

And probably they're about ready to plummet by the time you hear about them from your favorite TV or radio host.

If you look at the first three years of the best-performing stocks, they return about 150 percent for the first three years (see Figure 3.5). Then they fall off dramatically in the ensuing three years.

The moral: Don't just chase the winners because sooner or later the winners end up becoming losers. Even the best gurus get this stuff wrong from time to time.

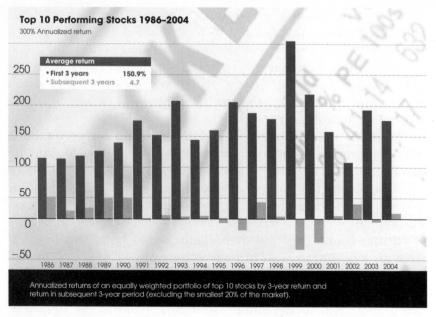

Top 10 Performing Stocks 1986–2004
300% Annualized return

Average return	
• First 3 years	150.9%
• Subsequent 3 years	4.7

Annualized returns of an equally weighted portfolio of top 10 stocks by 3-year return and return in subsequent 3-year period (excluding the smallest 20% of the market).

Figure 3.5   Main Street Chases the Best Performers

The truth is, too much trading may be hazardous to your wealth. Two University of California professors, Brad Barber and Terrance Odean, looked at 66,000 households dealing with a discount broker over a five-year period. They found that the most active traders earned 11 percent, and the average trader earned 16 percent. But the market, without any trading at all, earned almost 18 percent.

"Reverse Dollar-Cost Averaging"

Main Street also gets it wrong because people adopt what I call "reverse dollar-cost averaging." Dollar-cost averaging, as you may know, is a widely accepted way of investing. It's sort of Chapter 1, Verse 1 in the bible of financial planning: You put money into the market at regular intervals, buying more shares when prices are low and buying fewer when prices are high. And that's cool because you're taking advantage of the volatility.

But what I take issue with is taking money out of a volatile portfolio. Wall Street tells you to go ahead and invest your money according to an asset-allocation that includes large-cap stocks, small-cap stocks, value stocks and growth stocks, domestic and international stocks, and so on. That makes for a nifty-looking pie chart.

Then upon retirement, when you need the money, Wall Street tells you to take it out more or less evenly from these groups and then rebalance to your original proportions. That sounds good—but when the market is crashing and you're also taking out money from your stock portfolio, you'd be surprised at how quickly you can accelerate the loss and soon get down to next to nothing. It's like throwing water on a sinking ship—it just goes to the bottom that much faster.

For instance, here's a 25-year study that looked at three different portfolios—one of T-bills that were earning about 6 percent; another consisting of the S&P 500, which earned 13.3 percent during the period studied; and a third globally diversified portfolio that also earned 13.3 percent. A dollar invested in T-bills over 25 years grew to $5.72. A dollar in the S&P grew to $25 and change. And a dollar in the global portfolio also grew to $25 and change. (See Figure 3.6.)

But what's fascinating is what happens when you begin to extract money from these $100,000 portfolios in retirement. The T-bill portfolio would be worth only $31,566 after a quarter-century of 8 percent annual draw-downs. The S&P portfolio would have $232,200 after 25 years because it grew at 13.3 percent while you took out only 8 percent.

Compound Annual Return
1972–1997

- ### Portfolio "A" (T-Bills) 6%
  - One Dollar Grows to $5.72

- ### Portfolio "B" (S&P 500) 13.3%
  - One Dollar Grows to $25.45

- ### Portfolio "C" (Global Portfolio) 13.3%
  - One Dollar Grows to $25.60

Figure 3.6   A Tale of Three Portfolios
Source: Reinhardt Werba Bowen.

But—surprise!—the globally diversified portfolio, which earned the same 13.3 percent as the domestic portfolio, would be worth more than $891,000 after identical withdrawals. How can that be? In a word: *volatility*. You see, the global portfolio was less volatile than the domestic one. Thus, when it came time to take a distribution, the less-volatile portfolio lost less during the market downturns, giving it a much better recovery when the market rebounded. Or to put it another way, you sold fewer shares when the market was down and so had more shares with which to enjoy the recovery. Over the 25-year period, those shares were worth $600,000 more on just a $100,000 investment. *Stunning!*

That's why *Buckets of Money* works so well. Under the *Buckets of Money* strategy, you have a nonvolatile bucket of safe money—even less volatile than a global portfolio—from which you take your income. Stocks can go up, down, or sideways, and your income stream is not affected. Further, you aren't taking your living expenses out of a shrinking pool and causing it to shrink even more. You're not reverse-dollar-cost averaging. In short, you're doing retirement right.

Proper Allocation

Now, while I don't like drawing down income from a diversified stock portfolio, I *do* like having a diversified stock portfolio. Having large-cap, small-cap, domestic stocks, foreign stocks, and all the rest in Bucket 3 makes perfect sense.

But, in addition, you need certain asset classes that don't march in unison. You want certain asset classes that zig when others are zagging because if everything goes up or down at the same time, well . . . you get the idea.

So that's why I emphasize REITs, or real estate investment trusts. I like publicly traded REITs, but I particularly I like what are known as non-tradable REITs (which I'll explain later) that produce returns similar to stocks but don't march in lockstep with them.

You'll notice in the graphic in Figure 3.7 that 80 percent of the time Direct Real Estate, such as non-traded REITs, are zigging when stocks (as represented by the S&P 500) are zagging. And traded REITs correlate with the S&P 500 only 55 percent of the time. That's good because it cuts down on the volatility, on the extreme ups and downs.

What's more, studies show that by adding REITs you end up with a higher rate of return at lower risks. That approximates

	Direct Real Estate	Publicly Traded REITs	S&P 500	Small Stocks	Int'l Stocks	Govt. Bonds	T-Bills
Direct Real Estate	1.00	0.29	**0.20**	0.11	0.20	−0.10	0.26
Publicly Traded REITs	0.29	1.00	**0.55**	0.65	0.51	−0.10	0.02

Figure 3.7 Declining Equity REIT Correlation

Source: Reinhardt Werba Bowen. Correlation represented quarterly during the years 9/30/1989 through 6/30/2009. Direct Real Estate—NCREIF Property Trust Index; REITs—FTSE NAREIT Equity REIT Index; Large Company Stocks—Standard & Poor's 500, which is an unmanaged group of securities and considered to be representative of the stock market in general; Small Company Stocks—Ibbotson U.S. Small Stock Index; International stocks—Morgan Stanley Capital International Europe, Australasia, and Far East (EAFE®) Index; Bonds—U.S. Long-Term Government Bond Index; Treasury Bills—30-day U.S. Treasury Bill.

Note: Data as of June 30, 2009.

perfection—something akin to being able to find a double-fudge ice cream sundae with no calories.

As Figure 3.8 shows, a 20 percent addition allotment of REITs to a portfolio of stocks, bonds, and T-bills can actually increase your return. (I've been known to recommend as much as 30 percent to nontraded REITs as a bond alternative in times of lower bond yields and higher potential for inflation.)

And this is true of some other asset classes as well. So in the *Buckets of Money* strategy, we will put multiple asset classes in our long-term growth bucket . . . *and then never drain that stock portfolio for income.*

Proper Location

One other thing worth pointing out is the importance of *where* you put your stocks versus where you put your bonds. In other words, asset location.

Bonds pay interest, which is taxed at your ordinary-income-tax rate. It's best to have those in, say, a Roth IRA account where neither the earnings nor the withdrawals are taxed, or in some other type of tax-deferred account in which you don't realize the taxable interest each year. (See Figure 3.9.) Stocks, on the other hand, have—at least for now—capital-gains and special dividend treatments that make them better candidates for your taxable (nonretirement) accounts.

Stock and Bond Investors 1972–2008

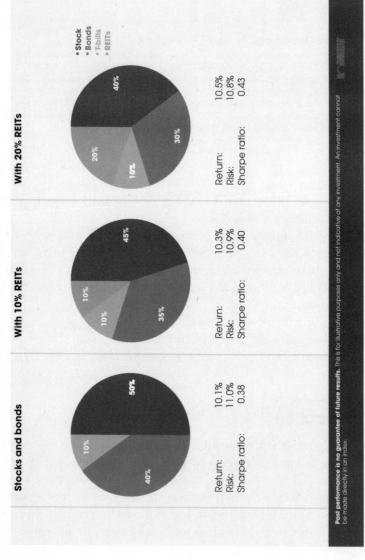

	Stocks and bonds	With 10% REITs	With 20% REITs

Stocks and bonds

50%
10%
40%

Return: 10.1%
Risk: 11.0%
Sharpe ratio: 0.38

With 10% REITs

45%
10%
10%
35%

Return: 10.3%
Risk: 10.9%
Sharpe ratio: 0.40

With 20% REITs

40%
20%
10%
30%

Return: 10.5%
Risk: 10.8%
Sharpe ratio: 0.43

• Stock
• Bonds
• T-bills
• REITs

Figure 3.8   Diversify to Reduce Risk or Increase Return

Source: © 2009 Morningstar, Inc. All rights reserved.

Figure 3.9   Allocating Between Accounts

The Federal Reserve did a study showing that we generally invest two-thirds of our money in stocks and one-third in bonds, but we're not always very smart about where we hold those securities. Two-thirds of our 401(k) money—which is taxed at ordinary-income rates when withdrawn—is in stocks and one-third is in bonds. Ideally, it might be the other way around.

In fact, according to Robert Dammon at Carnegie Mellon University, putting securities in the wrong type of an account can easily slice 20 percent off your nest egg. Of course, if pretty much all your money is in a 401(k), you don't have the flexibility to do this. But if you have taxable accounts, too, then keep in mind that you ideally want your equities and growth investments there and your bonds and ordinary-income investments in your tax-advantaged accounts.

An added benefit of stocks in a taxable account is that you get a step-up in the tax basis upon your death. That means when you die, the stock your heirs get is figured at its current market value instead of what you paid for it. So they don't owe taxes on the capital gains.

A Final Word

A key to successful, long-term investing is "buying" time and, by doing so, mitigating the risk. That's the basic premise of *Buckets of Money*—organize your investments into three main groupings (or "buckets")—and take almost all the risk in Bucket 3 with its stocks and real estate while spending down the first two, relatively "safe" buckets. This strategy can insulate you from the short-term ups and downs of the market while giving you the courage and discipline to stay invested and to plan your retirement years with confidence.

Now that we've gone over the basics of the *Buckets of Money* strategy and debunked many investment myths, let's take a more detailed look at what investments you can choose from and how those might work out in practice when you become "bucketized."

4

Choose the Proper Investments

Now that you understand the scientific underpinnings of *Buckets of Money*, let's look at some of the investments that might be right for each bucket. After that, we'll get into an example of how putting those investments in the proper bucket could work in practice.

Bucket 1: The Income Bucket

You'll remember that in Bucket 1 we'll be looking for unrisky investments that will generate income while we allow the other two buckets to grow. For certain individuals with potentially long life expectancies, a well-documented strategy is to add a guaranteed lifetime income annuity for part of Bucket 1. Then the balance of Bucket 1 consists of short-term investments to be spent down over a five-to-seven-year period.

Thus, this Bucket 1 can be best broken down into subcategories. Let's call them 1A and 1B, like so:

1A will be for income for life.

1B will be for short-term, fixed income.

A number of good choices exist for investments in either sub-bucket.

Sub-Bucket 1A: The Lifetime-Income Category

This bucket will be giving us lifetime income, and the only way to guarantee payments for a lifetime is through an annuity. (We'll examine annuities in much greater detail in Chapter 6.) Annuities are life-insurance products that traditionally have frightened away many investors because of their complexity.

However, it's increasingly clear that well-chosen annuities from credit-worthy companies can work wonders in your retirement portfolio. That's not just me saying that—as we'll see, scholars from the Wharton School at the University of Pennsylvania and others have shone new light on the role of the lifetime-income annuity. In fact, economists, who rarely agree on anything, are largely in accord that annuitization of a substantial portion of a retiree's wealth is a smart way to go.

For instance, an article—"Annuities and Individual Welfare" by Thomas Davidoff, Jeffrey R. Brown, and Peter A. Diamond—in *American Economic Review* (December 2005) says if you don't care about leaving money to your heirs or charities, you could optimally annuitize almost all your money. But even if you do care about making a bequest, substantial annuitization is still prudent.

"You should begin by annuitizing enough of your assets so that you can provide for 100 percent of your minimum acceptable level of retirement income. Annuitization provides the only viable way to achieve this without spending a lot more money," the authors state. Stocks, mutual funds, and fixed income, the study continues, are not substitutes for annuities because they don't address the major risk of outliving your assets. Nor do they guard against the risk of a serious stock market decline at the beginning of your retirement years.

Another study by David F. Babbel of the Wharton School and Craig B. Merrill of Brigham Young University says such income annuities can provide secure income for an entire lifetime for 25 percent to 40 percent less money than it would cost you to build your own level of lifetime income. What's more, by covering at least basic living expenses with income annuities, consumers gain greater flexibility and can take more investment risk with the rest of their portfolio.

In fact, data from finance professors all around the world tell us you have a very high likelihood of success if you annuitize a portion of your needed retirement income, preferably at least 25 percent to 50 percent. (To calculate how much to annuitize, subtract from what is needed each month the amount you'll be getting from Social Security and any pension benefits you're due. Then you can annuitize enough of your assets to provide for whatever level of monthly income you feel you'll need.)

Unlike the life annuities of the past, today's annuities offer many options. For instance, if you're worried about what would happen if you get sick and your money is tied up in an annuity, you can buy life annuities that increase the monthly payments by up to 400 percent when you reach a specific age, say 85. Other annuity contracts will give your heirs a refund of the money invested if you die. Annuities exist that will give you potential liquidity when you need it. Some allow you to invest in stocks for even greater potential income, and others can give you an inflation-adjusted retirement income.

But life annuities have disadvantages, too. In some instances— in particular with some of the older life annuities—there may be no residual value paid out to a beneficiary when the annuitant or the joint annuitant dies. Thus, if one (or two) die prematurely, that type of life annuity could turn out to be a poor investment. Also, with many life annuities there's no inflation protection whatsoever. So each year your payments are worth less in purchasing power. (However, as I mentioned, with some annuities, you can elect to have your monthly payments increase at rates ranging up to 6 percent per year. That entails significantly lower initial monthly payments, though they grow over time.)

A Recent Innovation.   One fairly recent solution to the lifetime-income need is something called a Guaranteed Minimum-Withdrawal Benefit Annuity (GMWB). With this type of annuity contract, an insurance company guarantees an income stream (usually 5 percent to 7 percent, depending on your age) of the principal amount invested for the rest of one or the joint lives of the annuitant(s). And that principal as reflected in the form of a death benefit can be inherited, based on certain restrictions.

The money is actually invested in a portfolio of subaccounts (like mutual funds) usually managed by the firm or a third party, such as Ibbotson or Morningstar. An Ibbotson study found that adding a GMWB variable annuity to a traditional stock-and-bond retirement portfolio can increase potential returns while decreasing risk. It also found the combined approach of a GMWB and a diversified portfolio produced a better result than 100 percent annuity portfolio or a portfolio made up exclusively of stocks and bonds with no annuities at all.

Here's how the GMWB works: The guaranteed-income amount is calculated on the account balance at the end of each contract year. If the balance is higher, the guaranteed income is higher and that income can never be reduced in the future even if the account balance subsequently drops.

For example, say you and your spouse invested $100,000 in a GMWB annuity that pays a 6 percent guaranteed lifetime income. Let's also assume the market does well and in a few years your $100,000 has grown to $120,000 by the end of a contract year. Your income base is now $120,000, thus the guaranteed payment for life is up to $7,200 (6 percent of $120,000). If it continues to grow to, say, $150,000, your guaranteed minimum withdrawal jumps to $9,000 (6 percent of $150,000).

If the market, however, suddenly goes into a major downturn and your $150,000 drops in value to, say, $50,000, that drop has no bearing on your income. The $9,000 annual withdrawal would be locked in for the rest of your life (and your spouse's life, if joint). In other words, the income can be adjusted upward if the account balance grows, but it cannot be reduced below 6 percent of whichever is greater—the initial premium or the high-watermark account value at the end of each contract year (or quarter or highest daily value, depending on the annuity). And, as stated, some annuities will return 100 percent of the initial premium upon death (subject to certain conditions), regardless of the underlying performance of the subaccounts.

Extra Cost.   Sound a little too good to be true? It *is* true. But, of course, you do pay for this type of insurance, and it's not inexpensive. You must figure about 2 percent in extra cost for this and other benefits of these types of annuity contracts. While on the surface that may seem a bit high, one must also factor in the risks the insurance company is assuming and the guaranteed benefits you are receiving.

Finance professors have pushed a pencil to these costs. A study done by Moshe Milevsky of York University in Canada concluded that the price charged by insurance companies for these types of benefits may actually be too low and cautions to be sure you select from among the very best insurance companies. I concur.

While variable annuities, of which this is one variant, may be right for some individuals, they're not right for everyone. Living-benefit variable annuity contracts are extremely complicated. One must always read the prospectus carefully before investing and take the time to understand all of the provisions in the contract. Hiring a competent professional who specializes in retirement planning is also advisable.

Bear in mind that a fixed lifetime annuity also can do the trick for Bucket 1A. In fact, you'd likely receive a slightly higher starting income payment. And you won't need to deal with the fees or complexity of the variable annuity. But, on the other hand, you won't get any of the upside benefits or the potential return of premium upon death.

Sub-Bucket 1B: The Fixed-Income Category

In this sub-bucket, we're looking for relatively short-term, super-safe, nonvolatile investments that will generate income. We'll spend down both principal and earnings while we allow the other two buckets to grow. A good number of choices exist.

CDs. Bucket 1B is money designed to be spent down over a roughly five- to seven-year period. Because you want to keep risk at a minimum, for a lot of people that'll mean looking at certificates of deposit (CDs). Offered by banks and brokerages, they pay a fixed rate of interest for a prescribed number of months or years. You're guaranteed to get back your principal as well as the promised interest. This has great appeal for conservative investors. In fact, you could ladder CDs to mature as you need the money, thus getting a higher potential interest rate from the longer maturities.

If you're a bit more risk-tolerant, you needn't focus exclusively on traditional CDs. For example, there are certain CDs insured by the Federal Deposit Insurance Corporation (FDIC) that offer returns similar to that of a stock index. These are called structured products, and they're sold by the big banks. They are the first cousins of the fixed indexed annuity offered by insurance companies. Most guarantee a positive return whether the stock market index goes up or down (subject to certain conditions). These so-called Absolute Return CDs (or barrier notes) are potentially good Bucket 1B supplements, especially when interest rates are low.

For instance, picture a goalpost or a wide letter H. The left pole represents a negative return of, say –15 percent. The right pole represents a positive return of +15 percent. Now assume you buy an 18-month CD. If the Standard & Poors 500 Index produces a return greater than –15 percent or less than +15 percent, your CD is credited with that amount of positive interest. So if the S&P does –8 percent, you'll earn +8 percent. If it earns –15 percent, you earn +15 percent. Or if it earns −6 percent, you'll get +6 percent and so on.

But on any day's closing if the total return goes below –15 percent or above +15 percent, the barrier will have been broken. The result? Your money will sit until the end of the 18 months, and you will earn zero interest. Your principal is still insured by the FDIC, but you would forfeit any interest if the S&P breaks the negative or positive barrier. When CDs are paying very low interest rates, one may be willing to gamble a small sum of interest for the benefit of receiving a fairly large sum regardless of whether stocks go up or down.

There's nothing particularly wrong with funding, say, part of 1B's income requirements with CDs or Absolute Return notes and then adding other investments that may have a little more volatility, or a little less liquidity, yet yield a potentially greater return. Below we explore some of these investments:

Government Bond Funds.   A government-bond fund is a mutual fund that invests in debt instruments issued by the U.S. government and its various agencies. This broad category can include U.S. Treasury securities (also known as T-bills or T-bonds) as well as mortgage-backed securities issued by government agencies such as the Government National Mortgage Association. Like all bond funds, government-bond funds seek to provide shareholders with a steady stream of current income from fund dividends. These funds are quite suitable for retirees and other investors who require a low-risk supplementary income source to help meet expenses.

These types of bond funds are considered the least risky because the government guarantees payment of interest and principal on the underlying securities. The great thing about government-bond funds is that the U.S. government is considered one of the most creditworthy entities in the world. In fact, it has never once defaulted on, or called, one of its debt instruments. Accordingly, a fund that specializes in U.S. Treasuries exposes investors to a lower degree of default risk. Also government-bond interest and, by extension, government-bond fund dividends, are tax-exempt at the state and local (not federal) levels.

But such funds are not without downsides. While the government guarantees the underlying securities, it does not guarantee that when you sell it before it matures that you will be able to get back all of your principal. If interest rates rise, you may get back less, and if interest rates fall, you may get back more.

If you buy bond funds with short or ultrashort maturities (recommended for Bucket 1B), the risk posed is relatively low, so the returns will usually be correspondingly low. As with any mutual fund, before investing in a government bond fund, you should carefully consider its investment objectives, risks, fees, and expenses, which can be found in the prospectus available from the fund. As always, read it carefully before investing.

I Bonds.   These are government-issued debt securities similar to regular savings bonds, except that they offer inflation protection because their yields are tied to the inflation rate.

They have virtually zero default risk and, thus, provide a safe opportunity for risk-averse investors with a short time-horizon.

I bonds contrast sharply with most fixed-income securities in that investors in traditional bonds lose out if inflation rises because the resale value of the bond falls and the interest payments don't buy as much as they used to. But purchasing an inflation-protected security, such as the I bond, you are guaranteed a specific *real* rate of return.

They work like this: When you buy the bond, you're given a fixed interest rate, usually fairly low, say 1 percent or 2 percent. (It has been as low as 0 percent.) Then, in addition, you receive additional interest that mirrors the most recent inflation rate for a six-month period. So as inflation moves up and down, so does the yield on your I bond. We've seen I bonds earn anywhere from 0 percent to a little over 9 percent on an annualized basis.

I bonds can be purchased electronically on the U.S. Treasury's web site, www.TreasuryDirect.gov, in increments as low as $25. If they're redeemed before five years have passed, the investor will forfeit interest payments for the three most recent months. This penalty is fairly insignificant compared to the benefit of the liquidity.

TIPS.   Another type of Treasury bond that may have appeal is the Treasury Inflation-Protected Securities, or TIPS, which are intended to increase in value during inflationary times. As with regular bonds, you're guaranteed a certain interest rate, or coupon, when you buy TIPS. But the difference is that the value of the bond's principal is adjusted twice a year to reflect changes in the Consumer Price Index. So if inflation rises, your interest payment is calculated by multiplying the guaranteed interest rate by the principal that's been revised upward.

TIPS are issued in varying maturities—generally 10 and 30 years, though they also can be bought in other increments in the secondary market. They can be bought directly from the government, through a broker, or through a mutual fund. There are tax implications, so talk to your advisor.

Immediate Term-Certain Annuities. These annuities pay a given amount per period (usually monthly) up to a specified date. They're usually bought with a lump-sum amount when you want to start taking income as soon as possible, usually at the beginning of retirement. The money that is invested in the annuity is guaranteed to earn a fixed rate of return.

If you die before the specified date (the term certain), the insurance company continues the payments to the heirs until the term expires. Term-certain annuities are often sold when CDs and money-market interest rates are low and individuals are looking for safe, stable income. Also, immediate annuities offer tax benefits, as every immediate annuity has something known as an "exclusion ratio," in which only a portion of your payment is taxed as you make withdrawals.

These types of annuities are very convenient because you don't need to constantly shop for CDs or worry about interest-rate fluctuations affecting your bonds. But they are no panacea. There will be times when term-certain annuities are competitive and times when they are not. Keep in mind there are no management fees or expense charges, but you will want your advisor to calculate your real return over the term certain.

Floating Rate Funds. For individuals with much stronger stomachs, a floating rate fund could be used as a higher-yielding alternative for Bucket 1B.

These funds contain securities with a variable interest or dividend rate. That rate is adjusted periodically based on the performance of another security, such as Treasury bills, or on the performance of lending rates—for instance, the prime rate or LIBOR (London Interbank Offered Rate)—that banks charge their best customers. For example, a floating-rate note might specify an interest rate that equals the current T-bill rate plus a certain number of basis points (a basis point equals 1/100th of a percentage point).

The amount these funds pay rises or falls in concert with the rate or yield they're related to. Thus, they tend to do much better than traditional bonds when rates are rising. Furthermore, they offer an investor the ability to adjust to changing interest rates without having to pay the transaction costs of constantly reinvesting in short-term debt instruments.

Adjustable-rate securities are designed to provide a market rate of return no matter how much rates fluctuate—within reason. Reason is often defined as not lower than a 3 percent floor and not higher than an 8 percent ceiling, meaning the floating rate usually will not fall below or rise above those amounts.

But most floating rate funds are tied to short-term loans to low-rated or unrated companies. These funds work best in a healthy economy in which the likelihood is that the lender will be repaid. In a struggling economy or a recession, companies sometimes default, and then floating rate funds can take a big hit. Many times these funds are reserved for Bucket 2, which gives them a little more time to recover. But for individuals unhappy with low-yielding CDs and an appetite for risk, they may be a good alternative. However, by no means should all of Bucket 1B be invested in floating rate funds.

A variation on a floating-rate bond is what's called a step-up bond, which pays one interest rate until a specified date (usually the call date). If the bond is not called by then, the coupon rate is increased, thus stepping up the interest payments. As with all bonds and bond funds, you need to work with an advisor who understands them and can explain *all* of the plusses and minuses before you buy.

These are just a few investment options for you to consider for Bucket 1B. Numerous others exist, including money markets and a host of individual securities. A good advisor can help you navigate through such choices.

Remember, the key to Bucket 1 is making sure there's enough safe and liquid money available when you need it. Thus, a CD or bond ladder, bond mutual funds or floating rate funds, T-bills or I-bonds all need to be relatively short term with maturity dates that match when you'll need the money. In other words, never go out long on your maturities when you need the money in short order. Short term for *Buckets of Money* purposes is five to seven years. After the short-term bucket is drained, it will be time to tap in the Bucket 2 money.

Bucket 2: The Relative Safety Bucket, Mid-Term Investments

Bucket 2, invested only slightly more aggressively, holds such investments as mid-term bonds, mortgage-backed securities, fixed and indexed annuities, and perhaps corporate and high-yield bonds. When Bucket 1 is depleted, you empty Bucket 2 into it for another specified number of years. Meanwhile, Bucket 3—reserved largely for stocks, real estate, and alternative investments—continues to grow.

To remain consistent with the science, it's not advisable to tinker too much with this Bucket 2. However, because there's generally a five- to seven-year horizon before needing the money, several intriguing investment opportunities exist:

Fixed Annuities

A fixed annuity is offered by a life insurance company that declares and guarantees a certain interest rate. These annuities operate as retirement accounts, which means generally that taking taxable withdrawals out of a nonqualified (meaning "non-IRA") account before age 59½ will entail a 10 percent federal tax penalty and maybe some state penalties as well.

So this is a contract between you and the insurer, with the idea of generating potentially better returns than other short- or mid-term investments. Many annuity products exist, and their names can be confusing. What's more, many financial pundits and self-proclaimed money experts constantly beat down annuities as an investment. They do this because most insurance company products aren't clearly understood, and most of the pundits haven't taken the time to understand them.

Fixed annuities are like tax-deferred CDs paying fixed, usually higher-yielding interest rates (compared to most money markets and CDs). As long as investors understand they are buying a contract that shouldn't be liquidated for five to seven years (due to a surrender penalty), and until after age 59½ (in a nonqualified account, due to federal-state penalties), they usually enjoy the higher returns and the comfort of knowing their money is safe and the annual returns guaranteed. Thus, fixed annuities can be a great complement to a well-diversified stock and bond portfolio, especially when interest rates are rising.

Fixed annuities, unlike variable annuities, for the most part are no-frills investments. They usually do not have extra fees or charges (outside of a nominal contract charge) and no out-of-the-ordinary expenses. They do not provide significant upside potential like variable annuities, no death benefits to speak of, and lack the potential to shift from safety to growth with one easy phone call in an attempt to maximize returns.

All of the profit the insurance company makes on the sale of fixed annuities is priced into the interest rate they credit. If you don't like the rate, you don't buy the contract.

I sometimes favor fixed annuities that lock in the rate for five to seven years (called multiyear guaranteed annuities, or MYGAs) instead of ones in which the rates change annually. That's especially true if I really like the rate and that rate can comfortably achieve my objective. This way the insurance company can't entice you with a high rate in the first year, and then once you're locked in, lower it to enhance the firm's profit. However, it is hard to beat a fixed annuity with a competitive floor rate (the rate cannot drop below the floor rate regardless of the interest-rate environment) offered by a company that offers its renewal clients the same rate as its new customers. In other words, they give their existing customers the same rates upon renewal as they are offering their new customers to entice them to buy.

To attract new business, some companies will offer big bonuses or unrealistic first-year rates to new investors, but once you're locked in they drop the rates on renewal. If the rates offered are the same regardless of whether it's a first-year rate for new clients or a renewal rate for existing clients, then you're reasonably assured of receiving a competitive rate of return.

I'm often asked, "How can insurance companies offer competitive, bond-type interest rates and little or no price volatility?" The answer is that insurance companies are in the business of assuming risk in return for guarantees. They take your investment dollars, guarantee a return consistent with the yield on most mid-term, fixed-income securities, and then invest the money in higher-yielding, longer-term investments (assuming the interest-rate risk and the investment risk themselves but also pocketing the spread between the two). Insurers have massive distribution forces, including agents, brokers, direct sales people, and direct distributors—all of whom constantly bring in new capital to be invested. Thus, going out longer on the yield curve to achieve a higher interest rate for their customers or investing in mortgages or private placements is not as risky for them as it would be for you or me.

Insurance companies can (with a few historic exceptions) weather interest-rate cycles. These firms, for the most part, use their entire portfolio to back their fixed annuities. In addition, because of a draconian surrender penalty, insurance companies know they will keep your money for the length of the contract term and don't have to worry about liquidity for at least a few years. This enables them to make more money for themselves and, in turn, give you more.

Most insurance companies' fixed annuities have constantly exceeded the interest rates of five-year CDs and 10-year Treasuries by 0.5 percent to 1 percent or more. Fixed annuities have long-term track records to prove their competitiveness over the past 10, 15, and 20 years. This makes them an excellent option for Bucket 2.

Corporate Bonds or Corporate Bond Funds

A corporate bond is issued by a corporation and is usually a longer-term debt instrument, generally with a maturity date of at least a year after the date of issue. Such bonds are often listed on major exchanges, and the interest payment is usually taxable. Sometimes these are zero-coupon bonds, meaning they pay no interest (coupon) but trade at a deep discount, rendering profit at maturity when the bond is redeemed for its full face value.

Despite bonds being listed on exchanges, the vast majority of trading volume in corporate bonds in most developed markets takes place in decentralized, dealer-based, over-the-counter markets. Some corporate bonds have an embedded call option that allows the issuer to redeem the debt before its maturity date. Other bonds, known as convertible bonds, allow investors to convert the bond into equity (stock).

Corporate bonds offer higher return than government bonds but at significantly higher risk. Like government bonds if sold prematurely in a rising interest-rate environment, the corporate bond could lose principal. But unlike government bonds, if the underlying corporation goes bankrupt, there's the potential for loss. Just ask someone who owned Lehman Brothers or Bear Stearns bonds! For the most part, if you stick with A-rated or better corporate bonds and diversify, you should be okay.

Ginnie Mae Funds

Ginnie Mae, or GNMA (Government National Mortgage Association), funds contain pools of government-backed mortgage securities. Their chief purpose is to promote home ownership by ensuring investor demand for home mortgages by buying these mortgages from lenders, thus allowing them to lend even more. GNMA is charged with pooling mortgages that are guaranteed by the Federal Housing Administration and the Veterans Administration.

Because GNMA is a federal agency, its bonds are backed by the "full faith and credit" of the federal government. It guarantees prompt monthly payments to its investors, whether or not homeowners in the pool have paid made their mortgage payments.

Generally, Ginnie Maes offer better yields than Treasuries, and they're an especially good choice when interest rates are steady, meaning homeowners are less likely to prepay their mortgages.

What's important to recognize is that, unlike ordinary bonds, GNMAs return a portion of principal along with the monthly income. This can make for a nice payout, but investors don't receive their principal back when the bonds mature. What's more, when interest rates decline, homeowners rush to refinance their mortgages. This hurts holders of Ginnie Maes because more of their principal is returned, and newer bonds purchased will have a lower yield. Mutual funds composed primarily of mortgage-backed securities also generally respond to interest-rate moves.

But they, too, are saddled with the same problem. In a rising interest-rate world, the values decrease if an investor were to need liquidity. And the investor receives less in principal refunds. In a declining interest-rate world, values increase but not for long as money from refinancing is reinvested at lower rates. Thus, in a volatile interest-rate environment, it's sort of "heads I win tails you lose." However, as stated, in a stable interest-rate environment, mortgage-backed securities can offer a slight advantage.

High-Yield Bond Funds

This is a mutual fund that invests primarily in high-yield bonds, also known as junk bonds because they have been given a "less-than-investment grade" rating by one or more of the credit-rating agencies, such as Standard & Poor's or Moody's.

In general, a bond receives a low rating if it's viewed as riskier than other bonds. This increased risk can be traced to the corporations that issue the bonds. Many are small firms without proven track records of sales and earnings; others are more established companies that may be experiencing financial difficulties. Some may even have a history of defaulting on or calling the bonds they have sold to the public. The common denominator is instability and questionable credit strength.

To compensate for the heightened default risk, the bond must generally offer a higher-than-average interest rate to attract investors. High-yield bonds are generally only appropriate for more aggressive investors who are comfortable with taking on greater risk with a portion of their portfolio in exchange for potentially higher returns.

When dealing with higher-risk investments, it can be useful to have someone who understands how to select individual high-yield bonds that offer the best risk-return profile—in other words, the highest return for the level of acceptable risk. Given the greater risk of default with high-yield bonds, spreading that risk among many different bonds can help reduce the impact of any one issuer's defaulting on its obligations. Of course, diversification alone cannot guarantee a profit or ensure against a loss.

Although high-yield bond fund dividends may provide income, they can also raise your income tax liability. If your fund lives up to the name "high-yield" and pays particularly large dividends, the tax consequences may be considerable, especially if you're in a high tax bracket. It's important, therefore, to look at a fund's after-tax returns (which can be found in the fund's prospectus, available from the fund). As with any mutual fund, obtain and read its prospectus, and carefully consider the investment objectives, risks, fees, and expenses outlined in it before investing.

International Bond Funds

An international bond fund is a mutual fund that invests primarily in foreign debt instruments. Depending on the fund's objectives, this type of fund might purchase bonds in many foreign markets throughout the world or might limit its holdings to a handful of countries instead. Likewise, the portfolio composition may vary in terms of the types of bonds targeted. Some funds focus exclusively on foreign corporate debt, others focus on bonds issued by foreign governments, and still others strive for a mix of the two. An international bond fund may also choose to focus on debt from developed countries, or emerging markets.

An *international* bond fund differs from a *global* bond fund, which invests in both U.S. and overseas markets. An international bond fund seeks to provide diversification as well as current income. Most of these funds invest in several markets around the globe, although the degree of diversification depends on the fund. As a result, these funds may be suitable for investors who want to invest in bonds outside the United States but want to reduce the risk individual foreign bonds carry. In addition, a bond fund investor might consider adding an international bond fund to her portfolio as a hedge against the U.S. bond funds or a declining dollar.

Many investors are reluctant to invest overseas (whether in stocks or bonds) because they are afraid of the risks and are unfamiliar with foreign markets. So these funds are only appropriate for investors comfortable with the unique risks.

Although investors should approach any overseas investment with caution, they may want to consider international funds (both bond and stock) for a small portion of their investment portfolio. I usually recommend that 10 percent to 30 percent of an individual's stock and bond portfolio be comprised of international investments. This diversifies the portfolio and balances out the other funds. If the U.S. bond market takes a dive (or if the dollar drops in value), one or two international bond funds might help offset the U.S. bond holdings.

However, remember that because the global credit markets are now more tightly interconnected than they have ever been, international debt may suffer along with U.S. credit markets in the event of serious financial problems. Also important to note is that due to the unique operational requirements of running an overseas investment, international funds may charge higher management and administrative fees than other funds. These added costs will, of course, cut into overall returns.

Fixed Indexed Annuities (FIA)

Another kind of annuity worth thinking about for your Bucket 2 is the Fixed Indexed Annuity (FIA). This is a hybrid fixed-annuity contract, meaning your returns are tied to the performance of the stock market. Unlike traditional fixed annuities where an insurer guarantees an interest rate, a FIA credits interest to the contract based on the performance of a stock index, such as the S&P 500.

FIAs are by far the most complex and the most popular of all of the fixed annuity contracts. Some brokers that sell them don't even know how they actually work. Like most investments, some are good and definitely worth consideration, and some are pretty much worthless.

The devil is in the details. For example, who wouldn't want a fixed annuity that paid the greater of (a) a minimum guaranteed interest rate of 2 percent or 3 percent or (b) 100 percent of the performance of the S&P 500 over a seven-year period? There's no way to lose if you're getting a worst-case 2 percent or 3 percent or whatever the market actually earns. Everything stated is true . . . but there's a little more to the story.

Sure, stocks should earn 8 percent or so over a seven-year time period. So this particular FIA sounds like a no brainer! And, if it actually did what this example suggests, it would be a very good deal. But before getting too carried away, let's first dissect this hypothetical FIA for accuracy.

First, the FIA doesn't really earn 100 percent of what the stock market earns. That's because the stocks in the S&P 500 return about 2 percent annually in the form of dividends over and above the actual growth of the index. Because the FIA doesn't return dividends, it will always earn at least 2 percent less than the market itself subject to the dividend yield at that time. This is not minor by any means. Over long time periods, dividends have accounted for approximately one-third of the entire return of the S&P 500.

Again, that doesn't make FIAs bad. It just means they're not as good for potential growth as buying the S&P itself. Of course, there's the tradeoff: FIAs can't lose money and, in fact, have a floor return, while the S&P obviously can lose—maybe a lot!

Further complicating the matter is how insurance companies sometimes calculate the return of the S&P index. Some contracts specify that you receive 100 percent of the S&P index returns based on a starting date and an ending date. However, in most instances you get 100 percent of the S&P subject to an annual cap of, say, 7 percent or 8 percent. Thus, in a year where the S&P does 15 percent, this contract caps out at a maximum return of 7 percent or 8 percent. Other contracts will average the performance of the S&P on a monthly or quarterly basis. This can also potentially reduce the overall rate of return over time.

Some FIAs pay huge bonuses up front as an incentive to buy them but then require the investor to annuitize the contract at usually dismal returns in order to collect on the bonus. So thinking one will earn market-like returns over long periods without the risk of the market is being delusional.

That doesn't mean FIAs have no place in a retirement portfolio. To the contrary, studies have shown that over long time periods FIAs have delivered returns of about 4 percent to 6 percent with guaranteed floor returns of 1 percent to 3 percent. This performance is similar to bonds, not stocks. During periods of accelerated stock market performance, FIAs have done significantly better than bond-like performance.

Jack Marrion, a well-known annuities consultant, says his research shows that both fixed rate and fixed index annuities have been competitive with CDs and taxable-bond mutual funds. For the 10 years ending in 2007, the 5-year annualized returns for index annuities averaged 5.79 percent, he said, outstripping the average taxable-bond fund return (5.29 percent), as well as the average fixed-rate annuities annualized return (4.73 percent), and the return of CDs (3.64 percent).

Thus, if an FIA is likely to earn about whatever bonds pay most of the time, but may actually beat bond performance some of the time, a competitive FIA may be an excellent bond alternative. FIAs, however, should never be used as an alternative to stocks or real estate in the portfolio. That's why it's best suited for Bucket 2.

Principal-Protected Annuities

These are new types of annuities that essentially eliminate the risks typically associated with variable annuities, whose rates of return fluctuate with the market. Principal-protected annuities guarantee— for a set period and, of course, for a price—that your capital will be kept safe. (They always remind me of Will Rogers' famous line: "I'm more concerned with the return *of* my investment than the return *on* my investment.") So these can be good for Bucket 2 investors who can't risk losing their out-of-pocket investment but want a shot at beating bonds or other relatively safe investments.

Most principal-protected annuities guarantee your initial investment even if the stock market falls. The underlying investment of the annuity still consists of mutual fund–like subaccounts. But if you buy a mutual fund outside of a principal-protected annuity, you are subject to the risk of the market. So it's kind of like an insurance policy on a mutual fund, guaranteeing your principal upon maturity.

So, like the fixed-indexed annuity, this one offers certain guarantees and the potential of higher performance without exposing principal to the market risk you'd face if you bought a mutual fund outside of an annuity.

The principal-protected annuity also gives you the opportunity to earn stock-market performance (including dividends but subject to certain fees). Unlike the indexed annuity, though, there's no cap or ceiling on what you can earn.

However, the floor return is not 1.5 percent to 3 percent; it's basically a return of principal. This type of annuity usually guarantees a return of your principal after several years as a floor on whatever the underlying portfolio does. Some even allow you to withdraw your gains or lock in a percentage of your gains annually— and that becomes your new floor return.

If the market performs in an average fashion, this annuity likely will produce bond-like returns. And if stocks plunge, you'll still have your principal guaranteed.

If the stock market does very well, this annuity may produce the best return of any mid-term investment, perhaps in the range of 6 percent to 9 percent. But because of the fees, it likely will never do as well as the overall market. So you're paying for the guaranteed principal protection.

To offer these guarantees, insurance firms charge higher fees than typical brokerage accounts. Annual fees and premium costs may range from 1 percent to 3 percent of the full value of the account. The typical holding period is seven years, and withdrawing money early (beyond the usual 10 percent annual liquidity) will incur surrender charges. And like other retirement accounts, taxable withdrawals and other distributions taken out of a nonqualified account prior to age 59½ are subject to a 10 percent federal tax penalty.

Beware of sellers of principal-protected annuities who exaggerate the benefits. For instance, an assertion that the fund "will beat

the performance of the S&P index" may be true during a bear
market when stock prices are falling. But it's clearly not true during
an extended bull market when stock prices for broad-based indexes
are rising sharply. Also, many principal-protected annuity companies can control the allocation of your account. So if the market is
going down, they can force you to increase bonds in your portfolio to reduce loss exposure. So careful evaluation should be done
before you purchase one of these.

Structured Products

I briefly discussed structured products earlier. These are special
financial instruments that offer greater flexibility and customization
than traditional investments. Designed to meet specific investment
objectives, structured products typically derive their payoff from
the performance of an underlying fixed income, equity, foreign
exchange, commodity, or index. Examples include buffer notes,
(which give you some downside risk protection or buffer), and
accelerated return notes (which give you upside leverage).

Normally with one- to three-year maturities, these allow the
investor to pick his time horizon, potential yield, credit quality, risk
tolerance and other factors. A simple example would be a five-year
bond linked with an option contract for increasing the returns.
Because profiles can be structured to pretty much match any investor's comfort zone, the notes offer a way of investing in an asset
class that otherwise would seem too risky.

Such notes can offer leveraged participation in the appreciation
of an underlying debt obligation (up to a certain cap) while provid-
ing limited downside protection from a decline in the underlying
security, commodity, or index. Investors forgo interest payments
over the term of the notes in exchange for the possibility of enhanced
returns at maturity due to leverage.

An example might be a note tied to the S&P 500 that provides
a downside buffer of, say, 10 percent. That means if the S&P were
to fall 15 percent, your note would only fall 5 percent. You'd have a
10 percent buffer. Likewise, if the S&P increased 10 percent, your
portfolio might increase 20 percent or twice the return of the
index, subject to a cap of, say, 25 percent.

These are very complex instruments offered by many of the big
banks. Such deals sometimes seem too good to be true. But keep in

mind these banks aren't doing this altruistically. Remember, there's always a downside whenever there's an upside. So it's advisable to get competent help before buying any structured product.

Virtually hundreds of options exist for Bucket 2—in fact, far too many to be covered in a strategy book like this one. But the key once again is matching the investment to the maturity date of when the money will be needed.

Because the Bucket 2 money refills Bucket 1 after five to seven years, there's lots of flexibility here. Please remember this bucket is labeled the "Relative Safety" bucket so most relatively safe investments, including those covered above, should work out just fine.

Bucket 3: The Growth Bucket, Long-Term Investments

The third bucket holds long-term investments that you're going to leave untouched for a period of years. This is where the growth in your portfolio is going to come from. So these are long-term investments that will fund your long-term liability—that is, your need for income for possibly decades in retirement.

But as was the case with Bucket 1, we should subdivide Bucket 3 to make it easier to understand and to fill. Again, let's use the divisions (A) and (B).

Sub-Bucket 3A: The Growth-and-Income Category

Bucket 3A is labeled "growth and income." That's because here we focus on growing our portfolio by emphasizing high-dividend-yielding investments. One thing we all learned from the decade that ended on December 31, 2009, is that growth stocks can be down for years—even a decade or more.

Thus, if a significant part of your return can come from dividends even when the market stalls for a period, you're still generating income. That income then can be used for spending or as dollar-cost-averaging that will rebound to your advantage when prices rise. While several different ways exist to achieve income and growth—such as high-dividend stocks, preferred shares, closed end funds, unit investment trusts, and royalty trusts—I feel the best approach is through real estate investment trusts (REITs). In particular, I like nontraded REITs. Because real estate and REITs are not as well known as other stock-like investments and yet I believe are best suited for Bucket 3A, I'll focus my attention on them.

Many think of real estate investing as too pricey or risky or hassle-prone. Or they think that just the really rich people like Donald Trump or Sam Zell can successfully invest in property. But the truth is, real estate should be part of every investor's diversified portfolio. One of the best ways to own real estate is through what are called real estate investment trusts, or REITs (pronounced *reets*).

Versatile investments, they're a lot like bonds because they produce income. And they're a lot like stocks in that they offer the potential of price appreciation. They also provide for possible rent increases while freeing you from the hassles of being a landlord. What's more, they complement stocks and bonds because REIT prices usually move in an opposite direction. A whole chapter of this book will be devoted to REITs, so I'll just give you the Cliffs Notes version here.

A REIT is usually a company that owns, and in most cases, operates real estate that produces rent. Almost any type of real estate holding—apartment buildings, shopping centers, office towers, hotels, warehouses, health-care facilities, golf course, even prisons and racetracks—can be owned by a REIT, although most specialize in just one or another of these categories. Some REITs invest in real estate–related loans, yet others own a combination of real properties and mortgages.

But here's what is common to all of them: They collect capital from investors and use it to buy income-producing assets. The REIT shareholder then owns a pro rata share of each separate property. The REITs collect the income (usually rent) and pass on the earnings to the investor in the form of dividends. And by law, at least 90 percent of the pretax income generated from the rents collected on the properties the REIT owns must be distributed to the shareholders. A REIT may also produce gains when the property it owns is sold at a profit.

REITs can be especially attractive because owning one is simpler, less risky, cheaper, and more diversified than buying property yourself. You get fewer hassles, less risk, and lower costs than actually owning your own income property. Also, while most of us can't afford to buy more than a few properties in our lifetimes, a REIT can own hundreds, resulting in much greater diversification.

Another plus for REITs is that investors can expect reliable and significant quarterly dividends, averaging 4 to 6 percent percent annually for traded REITs. Many nontraded REITs—meaning they don't trade on any exchanges and are only bought through an advisor—pay even more. In either case, the dividend is usually much more than you can expect from even the bluest of blue-chip stocks. Because rents tend to increase along with inflation, REIT dividends can offer protection during periods of rising prices.

REITs also provide an element of safety that some other investments don't. If you own stock or a bond in a company that goes bankrupt, you'll probably lose everything. But if you own a building through your REIT and your tenant goes bankrupt, you still have a building. Thus, even in the worst of situations, REITs have some advantages over stocks, bonds, and other forms of real estate.

Traded Versus Nontraded.   The one factor that really sets traded and nontraded REITs apart is the share-price volatility. Traded REITs are stocks that trade on the exchanges, and their prices fluctuate during the day based on supply and demand, just like the prices of any other stock as buyers and sellers bid. Most of the time the price moves up or down only pennies per share. Sometimes, however, the share price on traded REITs can be quite volatile.

By contrast, nontraded REITs don't trade on the exchanges and, thus, their share price doesn't change from minute to minute or from day to day. It typically remains relatively stable until the nontraded REIT either goes public, the REIT is priced for sale in the secondary market, or it begins to liquidate and sells its property.

It should be clear, however, that 18 months after a nontraded REIT closes its offering, the REIT sponsor is required to value all of the underlying properties based on a mark-to-market or point-in-time price. This could cause the share price to trade at less than the acquisition cost until the REIT has had enough time to raise rents and add value to the property. But because these are longer-term investments and the cash flow is unaffected by the revaluation, this is not usually an issue.

Nontraded REITs amount to direct ownership in real estate, and, like all real estate, they are long-term investments. Because they're not stocks that trade, they need to be priced in the marketplace for willing buyers and sellers. So if real estate prices soften, there's no need to create a market to sell and price accordingly. Instead, the investors simply hold the real estate, cash their dividend checks, and wait for the market to get better or for the properties to appreciate. Because the board decides when to sell or list, investors are not likely to get clobbered in a bad market as the REIT can simply hold on.

Sub-Bucket 3B: The Long-Term Growth Category

It's been proven time and again that stocks (and real estate and alternative investments) are the only major kinds of assets that consistently have provided over the long term a *real* rate of return—that is, a gain above and beyond the rate of inflation.

But not just *any* stock investing does that. Becoming a successful stock investor depends on how long you invest for, how diverse your portfolio is, and how you spread your wealth among stocks and other alternative investments. But once you've got your time horizon, diversification, and asset allocation in hand, you're faced with another dilemma: Do you concentrate on picking individual funds and stocks, or do you invest in the broad stock indexes?

This is known as the active-versus-passive approach, and each has its advocates. A head-to-head comparison between the two produces mixed results: Sometimes active managers beat their respective index or benchmark, and sometimes they don't. While it's easy to determine which methodology is better in hindsight, trying to figure out which will perform better in the future is another story.

When the markets are more volatile and smaller stocks tend to be in favor, the stock pickers or active managers usually win. That's because they can buy and sell stocks when they believe them to be under- or overvalued and invest accordingly. But when momentum and demand in the market causes most stocks to rise, indexing typically wins out over active management.

So deciding which method of investing—active management or passive management (indexing)—is better depends on how clairvoyant you are. My suggestion is to take a sort of have-your-cake-and-eat-it-too approach: Do both. Create a concentrated, active portion of your portfolio in which you strive for overperformance (alpha), and an index part that provides broad diversification. Some would argue that this is a fence-sitting posture, neither wholly timid nor wholly bold. But I would rather be half right than totally wrong. In both cases, however, I would rely on an oversight manager rather than attempt to tackle portfolio management on your own.

Even so, no money-management strategy is perfect 100 percent of the time. One investment strategy will outperform another sometimes. But you do need to *have* a strategy. This is one that I've used in my own personal money management, and one that I think will work well for many retirees or near-retirees.

It's important to remember that this Bucket 3B is totally separate from fixed investments and real estate. Stocks and alternative investments are for the aggressive, long-term-growth portion of your portfolio. And other the need for some occasional rebalancing, it shouldn't be touched for several years. All dividends (while lower than Bucket 3A) and capital gains are reinvested in Bucket 3B with a minimum 15-year time horizon. This should give the long-term growth portion of the portfolio ample time to smooth out the volatility of the stock market.

Value-Averaging.   One thing we've learned from history is that the best time to buy stocks is shortly after a bear market or a big decline. (Think of 2008!) It's just hard to get psyched up enough to buy when your emotions are telling you to head for the hills. That's why you need a disciplined approach to buying stocks in Bucket 3B. For example, let's say you expect an 8 percent annual return for Bucket 3B. And let's assume its value drops 10 percent in a year. At that point, it might be wise to take money from another source and force yourself to buy into Bucket 3 in order to not only make up the 10 percent loss but also add enough to equal the 8 percent positive return as well.

So if the portfolio did drop 10 percent and if you could afford it, adding 18 percent to your Bucket 3B portfolio from new contributions would be the thing to do. Otherwise, taking surplus money out of Bucket 2 and funding the 18 percent into Bucket 3B would get you back on track. Then, of course, in the future if Bucket 3 rebounds and is worth more than your 8 percent annualized return, you could replenish your Bucket 2 by using the surplus over the 8 percent amount.

Why 18 percent? Because 10 percent would make up for the 10 percent loss. Then you add another 8 percent to catch up to the expected 8 percent return. As a practical matter, this forces you to buy low and sell high. I call this "value averaging." It's like dollar-cost averaging, only better.

It means rebalancing your buckets by selling securities when you exceed your targets, and adding more to the buckets whose returns have dropped below your target figures.

The point is that the portfolio's value grows by 8 percent, in this case, regardless of the actual rate of return. When you do better than 8 percent, you sell some of the profit off the top. And when you do worse than 8 percent, you put more money into Bucket 3, either by adding new funds or draining a bit from your Bucket 2.

Other Possibilities. In addition to stocks, other kinds of investments lend themselves to Bucket 3B.

- *Oil and gas Master Limited Partnerships (MLPs).* While risky and volatile, these investments offer investors a simple value proposition: potential double-digit tax-advantaged yields and strong, recession-resistant growth.

  Unlike regular corporations, MLPs don't pay any corporate-level tax. Instead, these partnerships pass through the majority of their income to investors in the form of regular quarterly distributions. To qualify for MLP status, the partnership must receive at least 90 percent of its income from activities related to the production, processing, or transportation of natural resources such as oil, natural gas, or coal. Most commonly, the partnerships own "midstream" energy assets such as pipelines, storage facilities, and gas-processing facilities. They're generally "toll takers," earning a fee based on the volumes moved.

  In addition to receiving hefty distributions, investors also receive much of that income as "return on capital," meaning the taxes are generally deferred until you sell your units.

  MLPs are sold on the public exchanges, but they're long-term, complicated arrangements requiring special tax planning and a tolerance for volatility. Work with an advisor who can clearly explain the ins and outs. And keep your seat belt buckled because the ride could get bumpy.
- *Private equity arrangements.* By contrast, equity capital is not quoted on the public exchanges. It's invested directly in private companies. Capital for private equity is raised from

retail and institutional investors to fund new technologies, expand working capital, make acquisitions, or strengthen a balance sheet.

Private equity investments often demand long holding periods to allow for a turnaround of a distressed company or a liquidity event such as an IPO (initial public offering) or sale to a public company. Unless you're able and willing to put up $250,000 or more, your opportunities in this high-stakes world probably will be quite limited.

In fact, most private-equity firms typically look for investors willing to commit as much as $25 million. However, some mutual funds and exchange-traded funds (ETFs) exist that pool investors' funds to hold shares of many private partnerships and thus provide both access and diversification.

Also, keep in mind that most companies raising funds for expansion end up not being the next Microsoft but instead end up going out of business. So it pays to be as diversified as possible. And if you can't afford to lose, don't invest in private equity.

- *Royalty income trusts.* Neither stocks nor bonds, these are special-purpose financing arrangements created to hold investments or cash flows in operating companies. For instance, if an oil company has maturing oil wells with well-known rates of production and reserves, it might put the wells into a royalty trust. The company would receive a payout and continue to manage the trust for a fee.

  Royalty trusts are attractive to investors because they promise high yields compared to stocks and bonds. And they're attractive to firms wishing to sell cash-flow–producing assets because royalty trusts provide a higher sale price than is possible with conventional financing.

  Almost anything that produces income can be put into a trust, but oil- and gas-related properties predominate, both in Canada and in the United States. The units trade on the public exchanges.

  Royalty trusts also can be quite volatile, and if the pass-through tax treatment were ever repealed or became a political football, these investments could drop substantially overnight. Because MLPs and royalty trusts may produce high income, many investors are tempted to use them as a Bucket

3A investment. I would discourage that. Volatile investments require a long time-horizon and perform better when dividends are reinvested. Bucket 3A requires a more stable dividend and stable share price.

- *Commodities.* Trading in commodities—such things as corn, soy, hogs, metals, and petroleum—can offer a haven of sorts as a hedge against inflation. That's because commodity prices usually rise when inflation is accelerating. While investing in the commodities markets is a fairly sophisticated endeavor, commodity mutual funds provide an opportunity for almost any investor to get a piece of the action.

Commodities tend to have a low-to-negative correlation to traditional asset classes like stocks and bonds. But make no mistake: They carry higher risk than most other equity investments.

Trading futures is the purest way to invest in commodities, but an increasingly popular and probably less risky way of diversified investing in commodities is through commodity pools (limited partnerships) or commodity-related mutual funds or ETFs. The latter probably is the best bet for most investors. Such funds can be true *commodity* funds that physically hold the commodity, but they are more commonly funds that hold *commodity-linked* derivative instruments for those who don't wish to actually take possession of, say, the actual hogs, corn, or oil.

Natural resources funds also exist that invest in companies engaged in commodity-related fields, such as energy, mining, or agriculture. While they hold neither actual commodities nor commodity futures, they provide exposure to commodities by proxy.

What's more, understand that commodities markets of all kinds can be subject to wild, short-term price swings and long lulls. Over the course of just a few days, prices can soar to record highs and then plummet just as quickly to record lows. Before you invest in a commodity fund, be sure to read the fund's prospectus and annual report. Be sure you understand what you're buying and what role it will play in your portfolio. Similarly, pay close attention to how the fund's assets are weighted, and limit holdings to a small percentage of your portfolio.

Gold, in particular, is enjoying a resurgence in popularity as an investment. That's typical during periods of financial uncertainty. Many think that the metal—whether in the form of bullion, coins, the stocks of gold-mining companies, or funds of other securities that track the price of gold—can serve as a hedge against inflation or other economic disruptions. While gold may serve as a form of insurance against calamity, it doesn't pay a dividend or provide cash flow. Profits are made purely on price appreciation that's driven by supply and demand, and right now that demand is high.

What's more, understand that con artists and promoters abound in the industry. So if you're serious about getting into gold in a substantial way, you should commit yourself to a long period of self-education and find a reality-based advisor. This is not a world for rookies or amateurs.

A Final Word

Do you see the risk continuum? Bucket 1—with its *lifetime* and *short-term* components—produces income at virtually no risk. Bucket 2 is your relative safety bucket that'll refill Bucket 1 at intervals.

Bucket 3 is where you take the most risk. But even there the risk is mitigated by two factors: the lower-risk nature of the growth and income investments in Bucket 3A . . . and a long time horizon. Because the stock market has never lost money over a 15-year period, has always beaten inflation over 20-year periods (and since 1950 has produced about 8 percent or better return over 25-year periods), the stocks and other equities in Bucket 3B should grow over the years.

Now that we've seen how the buckets are structured and the array of possible choices, let's take a detailed look at how this might work out in real life.

CHAPTER

5

Execute the Buckets of Money Strategy

Meet Bill and Betsy Bucketeer. Bill and his wife Betsy have accumulated $1 million. (Don't sweat it if you haven't accumulated that much—or have accumulated a lot more. The concept remains the same, regardless.) Both aged 62, they each want to retire in four years when they'll get full Social Security benefits totaling about $45,000 per year. They'd like to receive a $50,000 per year income from their investment portfolio to add to that Social Security check. They save about $30,000 annually and are quite conservative with their spending. Both Bill and Betsy's families have particularly long life expectancies, well into their late 80s or early 90s. So Bill and his wife want to be sure they will never run out of money even if they live for several decades in retirement.

The Bucketeers' situation is somewhat typical, so we're going use them as our guinea pigs to see just how investing with a *Buckets of Money* strategy might work out. Of course, they're a hypothetical couple and are being used only as an example. Actual results may vary, and past performance is no guarantee of future returns.

First, Check Goals

The first thing we must do for the Bucketeers is to see if their goals are realistic. How much will their portfolio likely be worth in four years? Assuming they earn approximately 6 percent on the overall portfolio and add $30,000 per year from savings, their $1 million should grow in four years to about $1.4 million. Keep in mind that Bill and Betsy want $50,000 per year (in addition to their Social Security) in today's dollars. With inflation at 3 percent, they'll need about $56,000 per year, four years from now, to buy the same goods and services they can buy today for $50,000.

That $56,000 represents a 4 percent distribution or withdrawal rate on their expected $1.4 million. As numerous studies have shown, a 4 percent withdrawal is right in the "sweet spot" of predictability. That means Bill and Betsy can have a high degree of confidence that if they were to spend $56,000 annually (adjusted for inflation) from the $1.4 million portfolio (or 4 percent), that income should last a minimum of 30 years. Thus, all the numbers look good so far.

Art and Science

So *how* should they invest? There's both an art and science to investing. Art relies on the skills of money managers, timing, and understanding of global economics—plus maybe a little luck. Even so, it's still difficult to anticipate market-changing events and produce market-beating results. No one can predict the next devastating hurricane or earthquake. Nor can one predict a war or terrorist attack. No one can predict the next credit crisis, recession, depression, or other economic cataclysm. Each of those could—and probably would—wreak major havoc on the financial markets and one's investment portfolio. Even the most artful Picasso-like money managers could end up looking like a third-grader in art class.

A more foolproof way must be found to achieve financial success. It needs to be a method with a high degree of certainty, which, if implemented properly, will work under the stress of world wars, recessions, and the like. I believe it's possible to bullet-proof your retirement. But the key is found not in the art but rather in the *science* of a money-management strategy.

The science of asset allocation—in particular, the *Buckets of Money* approach—has been time-tested. We've lived through hurricanes and earthquakes, world wars, regional conflicts, recessions, depressions, and horrific terrorist attacks. As difficult as each of those was to deal with, emotionally and financially, the financial markets over the long run have always recovered. So if we follow the science of money, we needn't worry about short-term corrections or even a stock-market crash. We don't have to psychoanalyze the subprime real estate bubble or figure out when's the best time to sell short, buy collateralized mortgage obligations, or go international.

All we need is a plan that takes into account the fact that from time to time stuff happens that we can't control. Rather than stressing out about that, we need to expect it and plan around it. That's exactly what the *Buckets of Money* strategy does. It leads you to spend down your safe money over time so that you can invest your risky money without having to time the market, or study the market, or stress out about every single market blip. It follows science enough so that if you really want to juice up your portfolio with a more aggressive money-management strategy, you can do so as long as you have properly filled your safer buckets with enough money to buy time for the "artist" in you to eventually succeed.

Filling the Buckets

In building Bill and Betsy's buckets strategy, I'll be using some different vehicles consistent with research done by academics, finance professors, and papers written by numerous well-respected experts. I've written earlier about three buckets—Income, Relative Safety, and Growth. And that's the bedrock of the *Buckets of Money* strategy.

But in the extended example that follows, I'm going to use a slightly more sophisticated model, as we did in Chapter 4, that involves splitting two of the buckets. That's so you can see more clearly the gradations of difference between the kinds of investments. If you want to organize your retirement funds into three buckets or four or five, that's okay. The idea is still to have Income, Relative Safety, and Growth—but by subdividing the buckets I can better illustrate the benefits of different investment options and give you the flexibility of choosing those that best match your goals.

First, draw three buckets (two of them split) on a piece of paper. Number and label them from left to right:

1. **Income**—sub-buckets
   A. ("lifetime income")
   B. ("fixed income")
2. **Relative Safety**
3. **Growth**—sub-buckets
   A. ("growth and income," e.g., largely real estate)
   B. ("long-term growth," e.g., stocks and alternative investments)

Bucket 1

Bucket 1 is the Income bucket, and Bucket 1A is guaranteed income for life. This is usually in the form of an annuity, either purchased from a private company or a pension annuity from your company. As mentioned in the last chapter, academic research clearly shows that annuitizing at least some of one's income need produces the best potential results. Specifically, if you annuitize—that is, if you either have enough in the way of pensions and other guaranteed income or you purchase a guaranteed lifetime-income annuity (or a combination of the two) equal to 50 percent of your desired retirement income goal, you have a 96 percent chance that your inflation-adjusted 4 percent distribution will last at least 30 years. If you annuitize just 25 percent annually, you have about an 84 percent chance that a 4 percent distribution will last 30 years. And if you don't annuitize any income whatsoever, you have only about a 64 percent chance that your money will last 30 years.

That's a very compelling argument for anyone or any couple who expects at least one spouse to live well into their late 80s, 90s, or beyond. For reasons unknown to me, not everyone is totally comfortable with annuitizing income. I think some either don't like making a bet on their life expectancy or they just hate insurance companies. So not everyone will or even should buy a life annuity. Nonetheless, it is hard to argue with the science.

Because the likelihood is that Bill and Betsy will live into their late 80s or 90s and because they're conservative investors without guaranteed pensions, they're prime candidates for a lifetime income annuity. A good rule of thumb is to invest about 25 percent of your assets—though this number can vary with each person's circumstance—in a guaranteed lifetime annuity. So in Bucket 1A, let's place $350,000 ($1,400,000 × 25 percent) and fund a guaranteed lifetime annuity contract that produces an income stream of, say, 6 percent. That's some $21,000 of income annually. (This number may be higher or lower depending on your age.)

Bucket 1B, of course, is the fixed-income bucket. This will be invested in CDs, bonds, bond funds, and the like, that are designed to produce income for a five-to-seven-year period. Of course, at the end of that period is when Bucket 2 kicks in.

But let's not fill this Bucket 1B for now. In fact, let's not fill Bucket 2 yet either. Trust me here, and you'll soon see why we'll defer filling Buckets 1B and 2. Meanwhile, let's go on to next fill Bucket 3A.

Bucket 3A

Bucket 3A is for growth and income. One could use a variety of investments here, such as preferred stocks, closed-end funds, or high-dividend stocks. But I prefer direct ownership of real estate in Bucket 3A through nontraded REITs. Traded REITs are publicly traded stocks of real estate companies and typically pay a little less in the way of dividends than nontraded REITs. Plus, their share price can be quite volatile. As a result, traded REITs can be an important component of—and better suited for—Bucket 3B, the stock market and alternative investments bucket. There, slightly lower yields and wild fluctuations are expected in return for better potential returns over longer-term periods.

Because it's difficult, if not impossible, for the average real estate investor to achieve an acceptable level of diversification, I believe owning nontraded (nonvolatile) REITs work best for Bucket 3A. At the time of this writing, very conservative, multibillion dollar, low-leveraged, nontraded REITs yield approximately 6 percent to 7 percent. Ibbotson data tell us a 20 percent allocation to equity REITs produces a better return at a lower risk than a portfolio of just stocks and bonds. Furthermore, the stable income produced from a conservative, nontraded REIT portfolio is a pseudo-annuitized income stream. It can be used to supplement the annuity income from Bucket 1A. Or, if an investor has a much shorter life expectancy or simply refuses to buy an annuity, nontraded REITs are an excellent alternative. Also, nontraded REITs don't correlate with public REIT stocks, so they aid diversification.

So now let's fill Bucket 3A with $350,000 in nontraded REITs, the same amount we put in the annuity. That $350,000 is about 25 percent of Bill and Betsy's projected $1.4 million nest egg. (I usually like 20 percent to 30 percent. So here I split the difference.) Figuring an estimated 6 percent current yield, the annual income generated by Bucket 3A also should be about $21,000.

Why use nontraded REITs as opposed to getting all of your "lifetime" annuitized income from a life annuity? Because you're diversifying. It's important to note that the nontraded REITs are not guaranteed as is the annuity. But the REITs investment is slightly more aggressive—that is, it has more potential upside with a slightly higher downside.

For our purposes I'll illustrate both, paying out the income from the nontraded REITs in Bucket 3A along with the income from a guaranteed lifetime annuity in Bucket 1A. Thus, I would be essentially "annuitizing" about three-fourths of Bill and Betsy's required $56,000 income need. Doing so should give them a high degree of confidence that their $1.4 million portfolio will produce this needed annual income from stable sources. What's more, that income—along with some inflation protection—is likely to last as long as they do.

And because I like to follow science more than art, the Wharton study's number 1 recommendation appeals to me: "You should begin by annuitizing enough of your assets so that you can provide for 100 percent of your minimum acceptable level of retirement income." Thus, seeing Bill and Betsy cover 75 percent of their income need seems appropriate.

Okay, let's review where the Bucketeers stand with regard to annual income. Bill and Betsy will receive $21,000 from the life annuity (Bucket 1A) and $21,000 from their portfolio of non-traded REITs (Bucket 3A) for a total of $42,000. That means they're $14,000 short of their $56,000 income target.

Now that we know that, we can figure out how to make up the difference. So let's fill Bucket 1B—the fixed-income bucket—with $90,000. Our calculator tells us that amount, invested at, say, 3 percent will produce about $14,000 annually for seven years. (To calculate your own *Buckets of Money* plan, you can access my online calculator by registering at www.BucketsOfMoney.com.)

Planning for Inflation

Thus, with $350,000 in Bucket 1A, another $350,000 in Bucket 3A, and $90,000 in Bucket 1B, we've taken care for Bill and Betsy's income needs for the first seven years.

But we haven't yet factored in inflation. To keep the illustration simple, let's assume a 3 percent annual inflation bump to the income. And rather than adjust it annually (for instance, $56,000 the first year, $57,600 the second year, and so on), we can adjust it at the end of the seven-year period. So, again using our handy-dandy calculator (and a 3 percent inflation factor compounded for seven years), we can figure that the Bucketeers will need about $69,000 if they're going to be able to buy at the beginning of Year 8 what $56,000 bought in Year 1.

By the end of Year 7, Buckets 1A and 3B will still be cranking out at least $42,000. Having spent all the fixed-income in Bucket 1B by the end of Year 7, Bill and Betsy will be short $27,000 if they need $69,000 in income in Year 8. That's where Bucket 2, the Relative Safety bucket comes in.

You'll recall that Bucket 2 is invested in mid-term bonds, mortgage-backed securities, fixed and indexed annuities, and perhaps TIPS and corporate bonds. With a seven-year time horizon most, if not all, of the risk to this bucket is mitigated. Therefore, it can begin to be liquidated beginning in Year 8. Using a present-value calculation, we can see that it will take about $140,000 invested at, say, 5 percent today in those mid-term instruments to create $27,000 per year beginning in Year 8 and continuing through Year 15 (assuming a 3 percent return beginning in Year 8). Thus, Bill and Betsy can look forward to 15 years of inflation-adjusted income without touching their stocks.

So we can fill Bucket 2 with $140,000, and what do we have? We have:

$350,000 in Bucket 1A

$ 90,000 in Bucket 1B

$140,000 in Bucket 2

$350,000 in Bucket 3A

_____

$930,000 total investment so far.

Bucket 3B

We started with $1.4 million and have invested $930,000, so we have $470,000 yet to allocate. And we only have one unfilled bucket left, Bucket 3B. Thus, that $470,000 is how much Bill and Betsy can afford to put at risk by creating a diversified portfolio of stocks and alternative investments (such as timber, gold, commodities, and the like). Then they'll leave it untouched (save for occasional rebalancing) for a minimum of 15 years with dividends reinvested.

With this final bucket, we can get as sophisticated or as simple as we want. Personally, I prefer a combination of passive investments such as index funds and exchange-traded funds, known as ETFs.

But I also believe in actively managed, concentrated portfolios. There's definitely merit to hiring certain separate-account money managers who take advantage of different themes, including indexing, hedging, and overweighting or underweighting certain asset classes based on market conditions. Unlike mutual funds, these types of managed accounts usually have higher minimums, and such accounts with able managers can be difficult to find. But many do have a consistent track record of delivering alpha (excess risk-adjusted returns) at lower than average beta (risk). Retail investors tend to buy when everything looks rosy and sell when it looks bleak. Thus, when many mutual fund investors are heading for the hills or are in a buying frenzy, these larger institutional investors may react less to the emotions of the market and take advantage of pricing anomalies. This is why some observers believe that certain separate-account managers have consistently outperformed the indexes and their mutual fund counterparts over long periods.

It's long been known that most retail investors make the wrong moves at the wrong times for the wrong reasons. That's why so many successful investors became so by being contrarians rather than chasing the herd. This became abundantly clear around February 2009. Just as the market was bottoming out, many investors were pulling money out of stock funds at near-record levels. Soon thereafter stocks staged their best recovery since 1933. The point is that sometimes it's better to pay institutional money managers who won't chase the herd or move money around emotionally rather than investing with millions of fickle retail investors who make their decisions based on gut feel.

So having now filled all the buckets, let's see what Bill and Betsy's plan looks like and how they might perform in the years ahead.

When our hypothetical couple retires four years from now with their $1.4 million nest egg, they'll begin withdrawing $42,000 per year by taking $21,000 from the guaranteed annual annuity payments (Bucket 1A) and $21,000 from the growth-and-income (Bucket 3A). The balance of the inflation-adjusted income will be withdrawn from the CDs and the like in Bucket 1B. Each year they will take out of Bucket 1B the amount needed to equal the inflation-adjusted annual income requirement. Bucket 1B runs dry by the end of Year 7.

The Bottom Line

What's the bottom line for Mr. and Mrs. Bucketeer? Well, they will receive the inflation-adjusted $42,000 annual income from Buckets 1A and 3A. It's kind of irrelevant how well the annuity (which could be invested in a diversified portfolio of stocks and bonds) performs because we bought it for the guaranteed-lifetime income. So let's be conservative and say it only earns 4 percent, net of fees, and Bill and Betsy are drawing down 6 percent a year. That's a net loss of –2 percent annually.

But, still, that means they'll have about $205,000 left in Bucket 1A in 15 years—not to mention the guaranteed $21,000 in annual income they have been getting and will continue to receive for the balance of both spouses' lives.

Bucket 1B has been spent, and that's also true of Bucket 2.

Meanwhile, if the $350,000 invested in nontraded real estate in Bucket 3A appreciates over a 15-year period at just 2 percent annually—which is less than the projected rate of inflation—it should be worth $475,000. And if the $470,000 in stocks in Bucket 3B grow at, say, 8 percent—less than their historic norm—they should be worth about $1.55 million. Thus, the combined projected value adds up to more than $2.2 million, an ample sum that can be rebucketized, continuing the inflation-adjusted income.

The Fate of the Heirs

Just for argument's sake, let's say Bill and Betsy are driving down the road in Year 15 and are hit by a truck and tragically die. How would their heirs fare? Will they be richer or poorer than Bill and Betsy were 15 years earlier? To keep pace with inflation, their original $1.4 million would need to be worth a little under $2.2 million 15 years later.

Well, the heirs would inherit the annuity with a balance of $205,000 (Bucket 1A, invested at –2 percent per year for 15 years). They'd also get the $475,000 from the real estate and related investments in Bucket 3A ($350,000 growing at 2 percent annually), and the $1.55 million that may be expected from the stock and alternative investments in Bucket 3B, assuming an 8 percent return. The total? $2,230,000. That's more than what's needed for the heirs to have the same purchasing power that Bill and Betsy had 15 years earlier.

So the kids or other heirs would be left richer than Bill and Betsy, splitting $2,230,000 even though the Bucketeers only had $1.4 million when they retired 15 years ago. What's more, the old folks lived off the inflation-adjusted income all those years. *Sweet*, no?

Another Scenario

But what if the Bucketeers don't die in Year 15? Instead, they go on to live into their 90s, lasting, let's say, another a decade or more. And let's assume the worst—that the stock market didn't deliver the hoped-for 8 percent return over the 15-year time period.

Because the hypothetical 3 percent inflation has continued, they'll need more income then to retain the same purchasing power. A calculation reveals Bill and Betsy would need $87,000 a year to maintain their standard of living beginning in Year 16. So where is this income going to come from if they can't rebucketize the long-term growth bucket because the stock market hasn't met expectations?

The good news is that their annuity (Bucket 1A) is still kicking out at least $21,000 a year and that's going to continue risk-free. Their growth-and-income investments in Bucket 3A total $475,000. If need be, at that time they could simply pour that $475,000 into Buckets 1B and Bucket 2. Assuming the same modest returns from our first 15 years, that amount will be ample to spin off the additional $66,000 needed to reach the $87,000 income goal for at least nine more years. Meanwhile, of course, they continue to keep their hands off the long-term growth investments (Bucket 3B). Thus, they won't need to touch that money until the 24th year.

That's significant because, remember, during the worst 25-year period since 1950, stocks still produced an average annual return of 7.94 percent, very near the 8 percent expected return for Bucket 3B. So even if we take the worst-case scenario and apply it to the Bucketeers' Bucket 3B, they—or their heirs—will have $2,940,000 in stocks and alternative investments at the end of Year 24 ($470,000 invested at 7.94 percent for 24 years).

In other words, they started with $1 million, lived off the inflation-adjusted income for 24 years, and took almost no risk, except in the stock market bucket. That bucket, where the risk is mitigated by time, should grow—conservatively—to almost $3 million.

So if the Bucketeers died after the 24th year, have they left their heirs richer or poorer than the day the old folks were first bucketized? Well, let's see. If they started with $1.4 million, it would need to have grown to about $2.8 million by Year 24 to have kept pace with 3 percent inflation. We've already learned the stock and alternative investments bucket with a 7.94 percent return produces almost $3 million alone. So even if the annuity is worth zero in 24 years, the heirs still end up richer than Bill and Betsy after applying the 3 percent inflation factor. So the income was inflation-adjusted, and the principal was also inflation-adjusted.

That's the beauty of the *Buckets of Money* strategy!

How Much Risk?

Let's take a moment to look more closely at the question of risk. The guaranteed minimum-withdrawal benefit annuity in Bill and Betsy's Bucket 1A produced a *risk-free*, guaranteed $21,000 per year minimum income that could go higher (if the underlying account grows) but never lower than $21,000. Although the principal is not guaranteed, the income stream is guaranteed potentially for both their lives. (Even if the $350,000 originally invested lost 2 percent per year, after 24 years, there still would be about $66,000 left in the annuity.)

In Bucket 1B, the fixed-income bucket, little or nothing was risked because it was funded with CDs, Treasury investments, short-term bonds, and money funds. And in Bucket 2, the relative safety investments had a zero-to-moderate amount of risk, depending on the investments chosen. And any of the more aggressive investment risk was mitigated by the high dividends, seven-year time horizon, and the global diversification.

The real estate portfolio in Bucket 3A was a low-to-moderate risk, diversified portfolio of nontraded REITs with a stable income and a relatively stable share price.

Finally, Bucket 3B had a globally diversified portfolio of stocks with both passive and active money-management strategies using index funds, ETFs, hedges, commodities, and institutional separate-account managers. This portfolio, as all stock portfolios are, *is* risky in the short term. Keep in mind, however, that the risk is mitigated by the 15-to-25-year minimum time horizon (Bucket 1B and Bucket 2 together originally spanned 15 years) and the broad portfolio diversification. (Remember, too, there's never been a 15-year period, as measured by the S&P 500, in which stocks have lost money. And the worst 25-year period since 1950 still produced an almost 8 percent return.)

And, as I've shown, even if you extend the Bucketeers' life-expectancy—and their need for inflation-adjusted income—out another 10 years beyond that, their nest egg continues to grow at or above the rate of inflation.

How to Allocate

So how should the Bucketeers allocate the $1 million they have today? Simple. Just calculate the percentages of their asset allocation today based on the way the $1.4 million portfolio was bucketized. For example, if Bucket 3B, the stock and alternative investment bucket, represents $470,000 of the $1.4 million, that's about a third of the total. So they should allocate 33 percent of the current $1 million today to equities and alternative investments. They also should stay consistent with the other percentages so their allocation pie today looks something like this.

Funding these buckets now—four years in advance of actual retirement—based on the percentage allocation greatly minimizes the risk of a market correction or crash derailing the Bucketeers' retirement. Further, by applying this same asset allocation to the couple's annual $30,000 contributions, there's a high likelihood that the portfolio will look similar to the ideal portfolio illustrated for the $1.4 million sum expected in four years.

Allocating today instead of waiting also means there will still be reasonably safe, annuitized income in four years from the guaranteed minimum-withdrawal-benefit annuity and REITs. (Most guaranteed minimum-withdrawal-benefit annuities automatically increase the income base by 7 percent to 10 percent each year, guaranteed regardless of the performance of the underlying investments. This assures a higher, guaranteed income payment in the future.) That will be unaffected by a potential stock market decline (at least so far as the income), and if the stock and real estate markets do well, the starting income could be even higher. In addition, there will still be many years of safe and moderately safe money available to buy that 15 years of safe income, beginning when the individual retires.

The Importance of Bucketizing Now

The reason you should allocate your buckets now instead of waiting until retirement is that no one knows exactly when they will retire or need to get their hands on some income. Most of us have a retirement date in mind. But that ideal date may not coincide with our job situation or our health. We may be forced to retire sooner than planned and without having the buckets properly filled. Based on circumstances beyond our control, we could be taking on more risk than is prudent. Ask anyone who lost his or her job in 2008 and whose money was invested in aggressive stocks that lost 50 percent practically overnight.

Even younger individuals who are 10, 20, or more years away from retirement should fill their buckets as if they're retiring—or being forced into retirement—today.

Thus, a 45-year-old with, say, $250,000 should pretend she is retiring and forced into withdrawing 4 percent, or $10,000 per year, starting now. Then, bucketize accordingly.

While that person may not need to consider the lifetime-income annuity, the rest of the buckets should remain consistent with the plan. It's a way to create a foolproof asset-allocation model.

Once the *Buckets of Money* plan is designed based on a 4 percent distribution, then the investor can decide if that particular *Buckets of Money* strategy is too conservative for her time horizon. I would always tend toward the more conservative plan and bucketize the lump sum of my portfolio as if I'm taking the current withdrawal and reinvesting all of the earnings within their respective buckets.

However, in order to kick it up a notch, I might allocate all new contributions to the more aggressive stock bucket to take advantage of dollar-cost averaging instead of sprinkling the contributions pro rata among all the buckets. Likewise, a superaggressive strategy might be to not only allocate the new contributions to Bucket 3B but also the 4 percent income generated could be sent over to Bucket 3B.

I find this particular strategy to work best for younger, more risk-tolerant investors. It gives them the opportunity to potentially earn a little more. But if they unexpectedly lose their job or become sick and need to tap into their retirement money, they are already prepared with the *Buckets of Money* strategy.

A Final Word

In this extended example, we've looked at how a typical couple of preretirees might invest in each of their "buckets." Their financial situation may be different from yours, but the concepts are the same no matter what your level of wealth. And you probably share similar goals with our hypothetical couple—that is, to have enough income to live in comfortable retirement yet have some assurance that you won't run out of money in your later years.

In ensuing chapters we'll look at some of these investments in more detail and offer several acceptable alternatives for each bucket as well. Meanwhile, it looks as if Bill and Betsy are bucketized.

PART III

REFINE THE PLAN

CHAPTER

6

Take Another Look at Annuities

All types of annuities are being sold today because shell-shocked investors are seeking a guaranteed return on their money. Some may prefer a simple, immediate-payout annuity that provides a guaranteed income stream for life. Others want something as elaborate as a deferred variable annuity that gives them a shot at stock-market growth while protecting them from losses. Still others would like something between those two extremes.

Whichever, insurance companies are eager to accommodate with a sometimes-bewildering array of products. In fact, the chances are you may already own an annuity, should consider owning one, or will be pitched one someday. Yet with all the options available, buying the right annuity is not simple. So boning up on this invest-ment concept is probably a really good idea, especially to see if they have uses within the *Buckets of Money* retirement strategy.

What's an Annuity?

Here's the pure definition: an insurance contract that provides guaranteed income for a specified period, usually for the life of the insured. But that hardly describes the vast majority of annui-ties being sold today. They might better be defined as tax-deferred investment contracts with guaranteed benefits, such as principal protection, death benefits, guaranteed interest contracts, or guar-anteed income for life.

Basically, annuities come in only two types, *fixed* and *variable*. But the variations can be extremely complicated and difficult to understand. Even though an annuity is a product designed to provide reliable retirement income, it's often ruled out by the layman because it's so complex and confusing. Because of this complexity, many in the financial press have had a misguided view of annuities, and many investors have avoided them. In fact, a 2007 consumer-finance survey by the Federal Reserve found that only 5.5 percent of families owned an annuity.

While annuities may be exactly what you need as part of your retirement strategy, choosing the wrong annuity for the wrong reasons could be a big mistake. So learning one's way around annuities can be a big help to the *Buckets of Money* investor. And giving you that familiarity is the goal of this chapter. (A checklist at the end can tell you if you're a good candidate for a lifetime annuity.)

Getting a better understanding of annuities may actually change your view of them. I know it did for me. Like many financial planners, I was somewhat neutral on fixed annuities as a bond or CD alternative, and for years I was totally negative on variable annuities. But after reading all the research papers and doing my own present-value calculations based on various life-expectancy assumptions, I softened my skepticism. The older death-benefit annuities that I was most familiar with were, for the most part, expensive, and their uses were somewhat limited and not usually worth the cost. Thus, I was not ready to jump on the one-size-fits-all variable annuity (VA) bandwagon. However, lifetime fixed and VAs as well as the newer living-benefit VAs had some definite merit as shown by a ton of academic research, some of which I'll share in this chapter.

First, though, let's go over some of the background on the many different types of annuities:

Fixed Annuities

Fixed annuities pay the investor a fixed interest payment similar to a bank CD. But the simple comparison ends there.

Guaranteed-Payment Fixed Life Annuities. These are lifetime *fixed annuities without refund*—that is, they guarantee payment of principal and interest over one's entire lifespan or the life spans of the joint annuitants. Then, upon the second annuitant's death, nothing remains for the heirs. (The payout for two lives is somewhat lower than the payout for one life.)

Or you can get a life annuity with a refund of some, or all, of the unused capital if the annuitant dies before a certain period. That's called a *term-certain annuity*. For instance, you might buy one promising a lifetime payment with a 10-year term certain. Thus, if you die three years after the annuity payments begin, your heirs receive continuous payments for seven more years. A term-certain annuity has a lower payout than a no-refund annuity but continues payments until (a) the term ends or (b) the insured(s) dies, whichever comes later, and at which point the heirs receive nothing more.

Another variation is *period-certain fixed annuities*. These pay out 100 percent of the principal and interest over a specified period, not over a lifetime. It might guarantee payments over 5, 10, or 15 years. These types of annuities are very common in the cases of structured settlements. For example, say your child wins a lawsuit, and the judge awards damages in the form of a guaranteed payment of $30,000 per year for 10 years. In order for the judge to be 100 percent certain the minor will receive those payments, guaranteed, he may request this kind of annuity be purchased. The payments are guaranteed, so there's no risk of not receiving them.

Of course, it would be far too simple for all of us to understand if the insurance companies stopped at guaranteed-payment fixed annuities. Nope, there are others you also need to know about.

Fixed Tax-Deferred Annuities.   These types of annuities pay a fixed, tax-deferred rate of return for a certain period of time. For example, for a purchase price of $50,000 or more, XYZ insurance company will guarantee, say, 5.3 percent for five years. Or the insurance company may offer an interest rate of perhaps 5.3 percent annually over a term of seven years but your first-year rate is 7.3 percent (due to a 2 percent first-year bonus). Depending on the yield curve at the time of the purchase, surrender charges, bonuses, market value adjustments, and so on, the rate you receive on a fixed annuity may or may not be competitive.

I have found in periods of a steep yield curve—that's when long-term interest rates pay much higher interest than shorter-term maturities—fixed annuities are more competitive than bank CDs. However, in a flat or inverted-yield-curve environment, fixed annuities become less competitive. They do have an advantage of tax deferral until you begin withdrawals. So if you're in a high tax bracket today and expect to be in a lower tax bracket later, that could be a worthwhile consideration. Keep in mind all interest paid on an annuity contract is taxed at ordinary income rates and penalties exist if money is taken out of a nonqualified annuity before age 59½.

Unlike VAs, fixed annuities don't have ongoing expense charges or management fees. All charges and commissions are usually priced into the interest rate credited. So if you like the rate and the terms, you'll love the fixed annuity contract. However, early-surrender charges can be substantial if you cancel your contract before maturity, which is usually three to seven years. While most annuities allow for a 10 percent to 20 percent penalty-free withdrawal, you shouldn't purchase one if you will need any additional liquidity before the annuity matures.

Fixed-Indexed Annuities.   Fixed-indexed annuities (FIAs) are, you may recall from Chapter 4, hybrid fixed-annuity contracts that credit interest based on the performance of a stock index, such as the S&P 500 index. If the stock market falls sharply, a FIA provides for a 0 percent return in that particular year instead of a negative return. So they can be good for investors who want to participate in market returns without being vulnerable to market risk.

As a result, they're the most popular of the fixed annuity contracts because over the past few years investors have been seeking safer ways to grow their wealth with minimal risk to capital. Those investors have as their mantra "It's not what you make but what you keep that's the key." But such annuities are also the most complicated of the fixed annuity contracts, and depending on the fine print in the annuity contract, sometimes return less than what meets the eye.

A FIA provides a guarantee of principal, a guarantee of a minimum return over time, and the potential for growth participation typically pegged to a stock index—all on a tax-deferred basis. Typically, a FIA provides a guaranteed minimum return between 1.5 percent and 3 percent annually over the term of the contract even if the index remains flat or falls. So it doesn't have the market risk of VAs or mutual funds. And as stock indexes got hammered over the past decade, fixed-indexed annuities did quite well, making money in the up years and not participating in any of the loss years. Much to the chagrin of many pundits, fixed-indexed annuities have produced competitive returns.

According to one study, the five-year annualized return for fixed-indexed annuities averaged 5.79 percent, higher than taxable bond funds or fixed-rate annuities in general during this same time period. This has been true with a high level of consistency and only rare exceptions. What's more, the FIAs had a slight negative correlation with bond returns, meaning FIAs aid diversification and may be a good bond alternative or complement. According to the Advantage Group, a business-consulting organization, such index annuities provided 27 percent to 254 percent more interest than the average CD over a recent five-year period.

The mechanics of FIAs—how they calculate their index-linked returns—is very complex. What's more, many variations exist involving such things as:

The cap. This is the maximum amount of index-linked interest credited to the FIA. So if your cap is 7 percent of the S&P 500 index, and the S&P goes up 15 percent that year, you're still locked in at 7 percent.

Liquidity. These annuities involve contractual periods whereby penalties may result for early withdrawal. (However, many contracts allow free withdrawal up to certain amounts or in the event of death, disability, long-term care, hospitalization, or unemployment.)

Bonuses. Some FIAs offer upfront bonuses as an incentive to buy. But the tradeoff may be taking less favorable terms over the length of the contract.

Yield spread or asset fee. This is a deduction from the amount of interest earned to cover some of the insurer's expenses. For instance, if the index-linked return is 10 percent, a contract with a yield spread of 2 percent would net 8 percent after deducting the asset fee.

Averaging. Some contracts average the performance of the S&P monthly, weekly, or daily—instead of yearly—and that can potentially reduce the overall rate of return over the long term.

All this—and there's *more*—makes choosing a FIA quite daunting. Thus, I highly recommend you study any FIA contract very carefully before committing and only do business with professional advisors who can carefully and plainly explain all the details to you. Despite their complexity, FIAs can be a great way and a safe way to fill a "safe" *Bucket of Money* without any potential loss of principal and an upside as, or more, competitive as bonds or CDs.

Variable Annuities

More than $1 trillion is invested in VAs, making them the most widely sold annuities. Like fixed annuities, VAs also defer taxes on the underlying growth in the contract. But unlike fixed annuities, their returns vary with the actual performance of the subaccounts within the fund.

The subaccounts, which resemble mutual funds, may be invested in a myriad of styles, growth and value stocks, small- and mid-cap stocks, international stocks, all types of bonds, Treasuries, cash instruments, and so on. The investor can typically create her own asset allocation within the VA. There are lifetime annuities with variable payouts with or without certain period payments just like their fixed annuity counterparts. Also there are tax-deferred variable annuities with principal protection, bonuses, guaranteed income for life, and the like.

VAs also have penalty-free withdrawal provisions and surrender charges if the annuity is canceled prior to the surrender period. These surrender periods can be anywhere from zero to 10 or 15 years or more.

What sets VA products apart are the contractual guarantees and the fees you have to pay for them.

Death-Benefit Variable Annuities.   I call the older versions of VAs "death-benefit annuity contracts," and as a general rule, I don't like them. They work like this: Say you purchased a $100,000 VA. Assume over the next five years its subaccounts grew the portfolio's value to $150,000. Then suppose the market crashed and your VA was worth only $90,000 by the sixth year. The insurance company would lock in the $150,000 high-watermark value in the event you die. So if your death occurred in Year 6, your VA account would have been worth $90,000 but your heirs would have received a death benefit of the high-water mark value of $150,000.

So that's not a bad deal if you die at the right time, but not cheap either. These so-called death benefit VAs are expensive. I've long felt that the extra 1 percent to 1½ percent you pay annually for this and other benefits is not a good value unless you are older, uninsurable, and you want to participate in the stock market without it impacting your legacy dramatically if the market crashes and you suddenly die. You do get tax deferral, but I contend giving up capital gains and preferred dividend tax treatment as well as a stepped-up tax basis upon death in favor of ordinary-income tax treatment living or dead makes little sense, especially if you have to pay big fees to get it.

Living-Benefit Variable Annuities. A much better deal is the living-benefit VA contract. These come with provisions that investors can take advantage of during their lifetime, and although even more expensive than the death-benefit type, they may actually be well worth the price. The two most common provisions in a living-benefit annuity are the principal-protection rider and the guaranteed-minimum withdrawal benefit rider.

The *principal-protection* type of VA works exactly as it sounds. You get to invest your funds into an asset-allocation model (usually selected by the insurance company and managed by a third party, such as Ibbotson or Morningstar), and after a number of years (say, 9 or 10) you are, at the very least, guaranteed a complete return of your *principal* even if the market tanks along the way.

Many principal-protected contracts have periodic step-ups and reset the principal protection at the high-watermark amount. For example, let's say your $100,000 principal-protected annuity grows to $150,000 by the end of any contract year, then drops to $90,000 subsequently. Your principal could be protected at the $150,000 mark or some percentage of that $150,000 (for example, 80 percent, or $120,000) for the life of the contract. Thus, not only is your initial principal protected, the greater of your principal or high watermark, or a percentage of the high-watermark value, is protected.

These types of contracts work best for individuals who are older and afraid of any potential loss of principal but would still like to participate in the returns of the stock market. The all-in annual expenses can exceed 3 percent, so they aren't cheap. But ask anyone who owned something like this during the market implosion of 2008–2009, and they will tell you how much they love their VA.

Guaranteed-Minimum-Withdrawal-Benefit Annuities have a different guarantee. While the principal can fluctuate, the *income* you receive from guaranteed withdrawals can't ever go below the starting withdrawal rate. For example, say you invest $100,000. The insurance company might guarantee a 6 percent or $6,000 annual withdrawal for the rest of your life (and potentially the rest of your spouse's life). Even if the account value drops to zero or you live to be 120 years old, you're guaranteed an annual payment of no less than $6,000 per year from that $100,000 annuity contract. Furthermore, if the account balance grows to, say, $150,000 by the end of any contract year you are guaranteed a $9,000 withdrawal (6 percent of $150,000), never any less! If in a subsequent year your $150,000 account value drops to $90,000 you are still guaranteed 6 percent of the $150,000 high watermark value or $9,000 per year for the rest of your life, and possibly, the rest of your spouse's life.

Once again the fees on these types of contracts are high, but the benefits may be worth the cost. As mentioned in an earlier chapter, Dr. Moshe Milevsky, a finance professor from York University in Toronto, Canada, has been studying VAs for years. Contrary to the beliefs and writings of numerous pundits who claim the fees on variable annuities are excessive, Dr. Milevsky has concluded that insurers actually may not be charging enough for these types of living benefits. That's because life expectancies are rising, and with a volatile stock market, the insurance company may be on the hook to pay out benefits for a very long time with little chance to recoup its investment during a prolonged bear market.

Furthermore, what happens if the stock market has another decade like the late 1980s to the late 1990s when stocks grew ten fold? Locking in the principal or income based on a high watermark could be well worth the fee paid by the consumer, but clearly it wouldn't pencil out for the insurance company.

As stated, these so-called living-benefit annuities are more expensive than the old death-benefit ones. You'll pay about 2 to 3 percent more than if you just bought a regular, low-cost mutual fund. Most of the pundits and financial journalists loathe variable annuities, complaining about the fees relative to the benefits. I've concluded this is true for some but not all VAs.

In your particular case, is a living-benefit variable annuity worth an extra 2 percent or more annually? My take is that conservative investors who want an opportunity to potentially earn more than bonds may benefit from a VA with principal protection. That's because you can potentially dial the asset allocation to a model that includes both stocks and bonds. (Some insurance companies reserve the right to change the allocation during a volatile market.) If the stock portion does well even after fees, the VA should outperform bonds. If stocks tank, your principal is still protected.

For sure, individuals with longevity in their family history might be well served with a guaranteed-minimum-withdrawal-benefit annuity, a fixed life annuity and/or a variable life annuity. We don't know how long we're going to live, and we don't know how successful our portfolio will be. Your risk tolerance, life expectancy, and investment acumen play a key role in determining whether you should consider a lifetime VA.

However, one thing, as Figure 6.1 shows, is certain: People are living a lot longer. Remember, according to the Society of Actuaries, a healthy married couple age 65 has more than a 50 percent chance that one or the other will live beyond age 92 and better than a 25 percent chance one or the other will make it to age 97.

That could mean planning for income for 30 years or more after retirement. And as we've learned all too recently, a lot can go wrong in a very short time, not to mention 30 years.

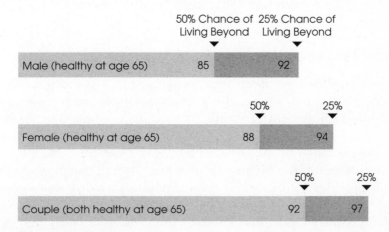

Figure 6.1   Long Odds
Source: Wharton Financial Institutions Center, "Investing your Lump Sum at Retirement."

Mortality tables also show that an average healthy American male at age 65 today can expect to reach approximately age 85. But because that's an *average*, half will live longer, meaning that if a man plans to cover his economic needs to the end of his "life expectancy" of 85, he faces a 50 percent chance of failure.

Predicting the Future

No one can predict the future. No one can forecast the next market crash, terrorist attack, subprime mortgage debacle, or act of war. Each of these, if serious enough, can wreak havoc with your retirement income. And none of us know how long we will live. A cure for certain cancers or heart disease could extend average life expectancies many years. That's the role of annuities: They bring certainty where there is usually none.

So for many individuals, living-benefit annuities can indeed be worth the price because they protect against both the risk of a market plunge and/or a foreshortened life. Note that Milevsky wisely cautions against buying annuities from less financially stable insurers. This is the same Dr. Milevsky who, in the 1990s, convinced many within the advisory as well as the academic community that the older type of death-benefit VA were not worth the fees paid for the life insurance benefits within those policies. He stated, and I agree wholeheartedly, that life insurance could be purchased far cheaper without it being bundled within a VA. But Dr. Milevsky now seems to feel there is indeed merit and value to some of the newer living-benefit variable annuities. He's not alone.

Good Evidence

Benefits of FIAs have long been recognized by a consensus of academic researchers. In fact, in a departure from form, academics tend to take a more sympathetic view of this product than do most investors.

As mentioned in the last chapter, there's evidence that suggests adding an annuitized lifetime income to an overall mix of stocks and bonds provides a substantially greater statistical chance that a retirement portfolio will last at least 30 years. A 2007 article on CNNMoney .com by Walter Updegrave cited an Ibbotson graphic suggesting a 65-year-old who annuitizes 50 percent of his retirement-income needs has about a 96 percent chance (given a 4 percent annual withdrawal plus a 3 percent annual bump for inflation) of lasting at least 30 years. Annuitizing 25 percent of the retirement-income need produces about an 84 percent chance the same distribution will last 30 years. And if there's no annuitized income, the potential success rate drops to about 64 percent. That's a pretty compelling statistic and bodes well for the use of life annuities in a conservative retirement plan. That life annuity could be fixed or in a living-benefit variable.

However, among the drawbacks of a fixed-life annuity is that if you don't live to or beyond your life expectancy, it could turn out to be a bad investment because usually there's no account balance for your heirs. Further, most fixed life annuities have no inflation protection or, if they do, the initial payout rate is quite low. That's why I favor living-benefit variable annuities with joint-life, guaranteed-minimum-withdrawal benefits. As with a fixed life annuity, you get a guaranteed income for the life of both spouses. However, instead of a zero account balance at the end of the second death, any remaining balance is distributed to the heirs after the survivor dies.

If the markets do well, especially in the early years of the lifetime payout, the insured could receive a higher payout, and that higher payout would then be guaranteed for both lives even if the account balance drops. Understand, though, that in most instances a fixed-life annuity with no refund will pay a marginally higher starting income than the guaranteed-minimum-withdrawal benefit VA.

What Academia Says

While annuities are gaining a lot more attention these days, still many pundits and even some financial journalists continue to preach against them. Perhaps they should listen to what academia is saying about them. For instance, according to a 2007 study co-sponsored by the Wharton School at the University of Pennsylvania and New York Life Insurance Co., lifetime-income annuities are the most cost-effective and least-risky asset class for generating guaranteed retirement income for life.

In fact, the professors, Wharton's David Babell and Brigham Young University's Craig Merrill, said, ". . . only lifetime income annuities can protect individuals in an efficient way from the risk of outliving their assets" and should be more widely used. Such benefits "simply cannot be duplicated by mutual funds, certificates of deposit, or any number of homegrown solutions," they added.

Specifically, they said, income annuities can offer financial security throughout retirement using 25 percent to 40 percent less money than would be needed to provide the same lifetime income stream by withdrawing 4 percent a year from a traditional portfolio of stocks, bonds, and cash. No other asset class can address the risk of outliving one's nest egg without requiring much more money.

Then a 2009 study, whose authors included Professor Babell and annuity guru Jack Marrion, used actual—rather than hypothetical—data and found that from 1997 through 2007, five-year-annualized returns from FIAs averaged 5.79 percent. That compared to 5.39 percent for taxable bond funds and 4.73 percent for fixed annuities. What's more, the FIA and bond fund were negatively correlated, which makes FIAs practically a separate asset class and thus at an advantage for asset allocation.

Recovery Strategy

As a case in point, let's say you had a $1 million portfolio that was ravaged, as most were, by the market meltdown of 2008–2009. So maybe it fell to $700,000. That really hurts! But you might be able to get a huge recovery bounce by using an immediate-payout life annuity.

For instance, you could take half of your remaining $700,000 to purchase that lifetime-income annuity. For his $350,000, a 66-year-old man could receive almost $28,000 a year, and a woman would get a bit less because of a longer life expectancy. And, of course, the older you are, the larger the payout.

So that 66-year-old man could continue to keep the other $350,000 in stocks, bonds, cash, and real estate, withdrawing 4 percent, or $14,000, a year, under a normal *Buckets of Money* strategy. He'd get $42,000 a year ($28,000 from the annuity plus $14,000 from the Buckets plan) in combined annuity payments and portfolio withdrawals. That's more than the $40,000 he would've been getting from a traditional 4 percent annual distribution from his original $1 million portfolio *even though his portfolio now has fallen by nearly a third*. It's that kind of arithmetic that helps account for a 50 percent rise in annuity sales in 2008. I don't normally recommend such a high allocation to lifetime-income annuities. But for those who need to recover from an ill-timed market downturn, a higher-than-usual income distribution may be suggested.

Risks and Opportunities

All annuities have their downsides. The big perceived disadvantage for immediate annuities has always been that when you die, the insurance company keeps the remainder of your investment. But, as mentioned, insurers now offer a variety of riders, including payouts to surviving spouses or other beneficiaries and one-time withdrawal or return-of-premium options.

If inflation is a concern, you also can buy an immediate annuity with an annual cost-of-living adjustment. You can usually opt for guaranteed minimum-income benefits or guaranteed minimum-withdrawal benefits. Of course, all such features reduce your monthly payout.

Be aware, too, that VAs cost more than fixed annuities, which have no direct loads or management fees. Long lock-up periods and/or high surrender charges accompany the guarantees, and how much of an upside the consumer gives up in return for the guarantee can be fairly steep. Failure to comparison-shop can be a costly mistake because the nonstandardized nature of variables creates pricing risk.

Because of the lack of standardization, understanding the exact terms of a product's guarantee is often difficult, even for some professionals. And long lock-up periods and high surrender charges heighten liquidity risk. When times were good, liquidity may not have been seen as important. But these days investors are more sensitive to the potential need to access their money. You can add a feature that provides liquidity, but of course that adds to the cost.

Particularly if you're inclined to buy an annuity with a guarantee (and many should), it's important to be aware of the complexities and dangers and to work with a professional who really understands these products.

Another risk—although I think it's a minor one—is that the insurance company won't be able to make good on its promises.

Financial strength matters more than ever. That's why it's important to stick with companies with conservative balance sheets and a long history of paying claims. In good times, nobody thought too much about counterparty risk, but it's more of an issue now. If the insurer has not hedged its exposure, the guarantee could be compromised. If the insurance company does go under, are the promised payments partially or fully backed by a state regulator? If you don't understand the contract, or if it can't be explained to your satisfaction, don't buy it.

What do these potential pitfalls tell us: First, it's important to shop around. Payout rates can vary widely. Further, it's imperative to buy only from highly rated companies and perhaps to even consider buying several smaller annuities from different firms as a way of diversifying.

Investors also may be well advised to consult a competent and experienced retirement planner. That's because the calculations can be quite complex to learn if a payout rate is fair. Payouts are linked to bond market yields, particularly those on government bonds. Government bonds yield little right now, so a planner should be able to give the investor a realistic picture of what he can expect.

A Final Word

You're right to want to "pensionize" your retirement savings over time. But just make sure you understand the ins and outs of any annuity you purchase.

Certain death-benefit annuities may be too expensive and not worthy of a place in your retirement portfolio. If you have one of those, you may want to consider a 1035 tax-free exchange into one with living benefits. As we learned from Dr. Milevsky, living-benefit annuities may actually be underpriced relative to the benefits and should be considered for many as part of their *Buckets of Money* strategy. Discussing the fees and costs relative to the features and advantages of variable annuity contracts as well as evaluating your tolerance for risk and family longevity with a qualified advisor may help you decide if annuities make sense for you. While annuities aren't right for everyone, they aren't wrong for everyone, either.

Checklist: Is a Life Annuity Right for You?

Instructions: Circle the answers to Questions 1 through 8 that best describe you. Total your score at the end.

1. Do you or your spouse expect to live beyond the age of 90?

   Yes—5   No—0

2. Are you a conservative investor?

   Yes—5   Moderate—3   Aggressive—1

3. As far as leaving your children an inheritance you believe:

   If they get anything that's great, but not if it affects your current lifestyle—5

   You would like to leave them something, but it's not a high priority—3

   You want to leave them the maximum amount—1

4. Do you consider yourself a . . .

   Novice investor—5

   Average investor—3

   Excellent investor—1

5. Your pensions and Social Security represent . . .

   Less than 25 percent of your retirement income need—5

   Less than 50 percent of your retirement income need—3

   More than 50 percent of your retirement income need—1

6. You want to take a distribution of . . .

   More than 4 percent from your investment portfolio—5

   4 percent or less from your investment portfolio—3

   Nothing, I don't need to take anything at retirement—1

7. Your age is . . .

   Over 59½—5   Between 50 and 59½—3   Under 50—1

8. You believe the stock market will produce returns of:

   8 percent + — 5   6–8 percent —3   Less than 6 percent—1

Continued

Scoring

If you got 25 or more points, you're a definite candidate.

If you scored 18–24, careful consideration is in order. Talk to a competent advisor.

Less than 18: You're probably not a candidate.

A final note: If you decide to purchase a life annuity, I usually recommend you invest no more than 25 percent of your investment portfolio unless your income needs are greater than a 4 percent or 5 percent distribution rate.

7

See What REITs Can Do for You

"Location. Location. Location." That's the oft-heard mantra of the real estate investor. And that's good as far as it goes. But a better cry for the *Buckets of Money* investor might be "Diversification. Diversification. Diversification." That's because there's no better tool for real-estate diversification than what are called nontraded Real Estate Investment Trusts (REITs). They're one of the best-kept cash-flow secrets and least-understood growth-and-income investments. Because of this, I'll do my best in this chapter to cover in detail what they are, how they work, why they're not particularly liked by Wall Street, and, of course, why they're a great investment for Bucket 3A.

Nontraded REITs combine the stability and yield of a bond with the appreciation potential of a stock. Thus, low- to moderately-leveraged nontraded REITs, which I'll describe shortly, may be an excellent choice to add to the annuitized-income part of your *Buckets of Money* plan.

It's true that real estate suffered a blow to its image in 2008–2009. But by its nature real estate is cyclical, and the aftermath of the meltdown may well offer exceptional opportunities.

We touched on REITs in Chapters 4 and 5, but in this chapter we'll dig into more detail, especially about nontraded REITs. As you may recall, REITs can provide many investors with:

- A stable income stream from diversified property holdings
- Appreciation as the per-share price of a REIT rises
- Dividend growth that can create a hedge against inflation

- Professional property management so you don't need to be the landlord
- A complement to stocks and bonds because REIT prices usually move in an opposite direction
- A "pass through" of property depreciation that means 30 percent to 50 percent of REIT income is tax-deferred

What Exactly Is a REIT?

A REIT usually owns and, in most cases, operates some kind of real estate that produces income. That could be apartment buildings, shopping centers, office towers, hotels, warehouses, health-care facilities, or what have you. Yet other REITs invest in real-estate–related loans, or own a combination of real properties and mortgages.

All of them pool money from investors to buy income-producing properties. Basically, the REIT shareholder then owns a pro rata share of each separate property. The REITs collect the income (rent) and then pass on the earnings to investors in the form of dividends. A REIT also earns money when it sells property at a profit.

Combining the Best Features

Congress created REITs in 1960 to give anyone the ability to invest in large-scale commercial properties. The industry has grown dramatically in size and importance since then. REITs now operate in nearly every major metropolitan area and in several foreign locations.

To qualify as a REIT and thus avoid paying corporate taxes, a REIT—whether traded or nontraded—must have at least 100 investors and agree to pass at least 90 percent of its taxable income onto its shareholders each year. In fact, most remit 100 percent of their taxable income to shareholders, and thus owe no corporate income tax.

A REIT, like all public companies, must be managed by an independent board of directors or trustees. It also must have at least 75 percent of its assets invested in real estate, and have less than 50 percent of its outstanding shares concentrated in the hands of five or fewer shareholders. It must provide investors with prospectuses, annual reports, and other periodic updates as well as comply with all rules and regulations set forth by the Securities and Exchange Commission (SEC) and the Financial Industry Regulatory Authority (FINRA).

REITs give an investor a practical, effective way to include professionally managed real estate in a diversified investment portfolio. In fact, in many ways, when you invest in a REIT, you get the best features of real estate, stocks, and bonds. Why?

- *Because there's less risk and hassle than when buying and maintaining property yourself.* You get professional property management without the headaches of being a landlord. And because a REIT owns many properties, you face less risk that trouble at one site will significantly affect you.
- *Because the total performance is better.* According to the National Association of Real Estate Investment Trusts, compound annual REIT returns for the 30 years from 1975 to 2005 were 13.8 percent. That compares to 8.8 percent for the Dow Jones Industrial Average, 10.9 percent for the NASDAQ, and 12.7 percent for the S&P 500 Index.
- *Because you get better dividends.* Investors can expect dividends averaging 4 percent to 6 percent annually for public REITs, or roughly four times those of other stocks, on average. Many nontraded REITs pay even more. And the fact that REITs can raise rents gives you some protection during inflationary periods.
- *Because adding REITs to your portfolio can lessen its volatility.* They often move in opposite directions from stocks and bonds, thus reducing overall fluctuation.
- *Because you get safety that even corporate bonds can't provide.* While REITs are often compared to bonds because of the stability of their income, they offer key advantages over bonds.

To understand, consider this example:

Let's say you can buy a 30-year, $10,000 bond issued by the XYZ Corp., one of America's oldest and most respected firms. Or you buy a REIT that owns the building where XYZ has its headquarters.

Scenario A—The company prospers

XYZ Corp. does well. With your bond, you can expect to get regular interest payments at a fixed rate. And the end of the 30 years, you'll get your $10,000 back.

With a REIT, the headquarters building appreciates. As a result, the REIT may increase in price because the value of its property has grown. What's more, you get credit for the building's depreciation, reducing the taxes on some of your REIT income. And yet another plus: If XYZ Corp. has a cost-of-living adjustment in its lease with the REIT, you—unlike the bondholders—can expect increased income each year as XYZ's rent goes up.

Scenario B—The company stumbles

Who knows what could go wrong? Maybe a problem with an XYZ product spawns a flood of horrendously costly liability suits. Or maybe there's war overseas where XYZ has its factories. Or perhaps Congress passes a law that cripples this particular industry. The possibilities abound.

But, in any event, XYZ's profits dip. Maybe it even starts losing money.

What happens to the bond? Well, its price will fall. Investors will shy away from XYZ debt because of the firm's reduced capacity to repay. You will still get your interest payments, but if you sell the bond before it matures, you'll probably take a loss.

What happens to the REIT? XYZ, despite its woes, still needs a building for its headquarters. And it still needs to pay rent to your REIT. In fact, XYZ is obligated to pay such operating expenses *before* making interest payments to bondholders or dividends to stockholders. So the rent it pays to the REIT gets top priority. (As with the bond, though, selling a REIT prematurely or in a down market most likely would result in a loss.)

Scenario C—The company goes bankrupt

Let's say the bad news just keeps on coming. Maybe the liability suits overwhelm the company, the war completely shuts down XYZ's factories, or the Congressional action proves fatal. XYZ files for bankruptcy.

Stockholders will almost certainly get nothing, and bondholders probably would see their interest payments stop and, in a worst-case scenario, might lose their principal, too. What about the REIT?

Well, it still owns the building. And XYZ, if it's functioning at all, still needs to pay its rent. Particularly if the REIT is low-leveraged (meaning, it has very little debt), its overhead is low. Thus, it remains in a good position to keep paying all or at least some of its dividend to you, the REIT shareholder. By owning the building with little debt, a low-leveraged REIT can still make money by collecting some or all of the rent due from XYZ or by seeking a new tenant for the building. Take the case of Enron. Remember its beautiful office building in Houston marked by the distinctive crooked "E" sign? The firm, of course, went bankrupt, but the building owners have been able to re-lease the building because the real estate is good, well-located, and affordable.

So, in summary, if you own a bond and the underlying company goes bankrupt, you could lose everything. If you own a building and your tenant goes bankrupt, you still have a building. Thus, even in the worst of situations, REITs—particularly a combination of well-diversified, low-leveraged, and moderately leveraged ones—have some advantages over stocks, bonds, and other forms of real estate.

However, REITs should never be used to replace bonds in your portfolio. The comparison cited here is strictly to illustrate the advantages of REITs. A balance of stocks, bonds, cash, and real estate is how savvy investors diversify. (Just to be doubly clear: Bonds and bond alternatives, such as fixed indexed annuities, can be Bucket 2, mid-term investments. REITs are Bucket 3, long-term investments.)

Public versus Nontraded REITS

There are about 300 REITs, which together own perhaps $400 billion in assets. More than half of them—known as *public* or *traded* REITs—can be bought and sold just like stocks. You trade them through a stockbroker or through a discount brokerage. You can also buy and sell public REITs through a mutual fund.

Public REITs are very liquid. But it's both good and bad news that these shares trade freely. That's because they fluctuate, just like any other stock. While buying public REITs gives you property ownership and may produce a good income, owning them doesn't shield you from the extreme ups and downs of the market.

That's why nontraded, or private, REITs may be preferable for some investors. They are purchased through a financial advisor and require more of a long-term commitment because they don't trade as readily. (Many nontraded REITs allow investors to redeem shares once a quarter, subject to certain requirements.)

Particularly desirable are nontraded REITs that are *low-leveraged*, or *moderately leveraged*, meaning they don't carry enormous debt and thus have fewer fixed costs and more flexibility. Thus, even in difficult times, a low-leveraged REIT may have to cut its dividend, but it's not likely you will lose your principal sum.

Because they're not being traded, nontraded REITs don't fluctuate daily in price. They are usually private en route to becoming a listed, or public, company, or the properties are scheduled to be sold in the marketplace. While less liquid, they fit nicely into a long-term growth and income bucket.

Another Advantage

Here's another big advantage of nontraded REITs: Often they're in the growth stage, still raising money from investors and acquiring properties, such as commercial buildings, hotels, industrial parks, apartments, and assisted-living facilities. They're competing with public REITs for those properties and for really good tenants.

The capital that flows in from financial advisors gives private REITs a leg up. Why? Because the public REIT, whose shares are being traded on the stock exchanges, may not be getting any new inflows of investor cash. It can raise money by borrowing, which raises the risk. Or it can issue new shares, which can be very costly because the big investment banks don't handle those types of offerings for free. Such new shares also dilute the existing shareholders. And either route—borrowing or issuing new shares—takes time and costs money.

So it's conceivable a nontraded REITs is likely to be in a better position to get the best deal and achieve the most diversification. The nontraded REIT, with a large, growing influx of cash may be better able to acquire multiple properties at a good price and close the deals quickly.

Traditionally, public REITs sometimes lack the access to capital when great acquisition opportunities appear, such as after the 9/11 terrorist attacks or during the 2008–2009 real estate meltdown. In the aftermath of those events, real estate prices plummeted. If you had access to a lot of cash, you could buy properties at discounted prices. The appetite on Wall Street for new offerings to raise capital for public REITs was almost nonexistent then. Meanwhile, the nontraded REITs, not reliant on Wall Street, were still raising cash, and as a result, were able to close more quickly—in weeks, say, instead of months. Not having cash or facing high borrowing costs can be the difference between a deal with good economics or just average economics. This may give a slight edge to nontraded REITs that are constantly raising cash and attempting to make money by making good acquisitions.

Also, size matters. Most public REITs are small compared to their nontraded counterparts. To achieve the type of diversification I seek for stability of income and long-term growth, you need a REIT with billions of dollars invested. Most public REITs are small compared to the behemoth $2 billion to $5 billion nontraded REITs that exist today.

But that's not to say that public REITs don't have advantages. Instant liquidity gives some investors the comfort of knowing they can sell their REIT shares at any time. Many public REITs have long-standing track records of having successfully bought real estate and have access to large sums of money through lines of credit or new offerings. So public REITs also can provide excellent diversification and should be part of your investment plan for long-term growth but as part of the stock category, not the growth-and-income category. As Morningstar has pointed out, while diversification "does not eliminate the risk of investment loss, adding assets with low correlation may soften the impact of market swings because they do not all react to economic and market conditions in the exact same manner."

The *Buckets of Money* strategy includes owning a few nontraded REITs for income and growth as well as an index fund of public REITs or an exchange-traded fund (ETF) or managed REIT mutual fund in the stock category. While the dividends may be distributed for income from the nontraded REITs, public REIT dividends should be reinvested to take advantage of the volatility. This combination gives the investor real estate diversification as well as income and conservative growth along with the long-term growth potential of real estate stocks.

I'll talk more about this dual-REIT strategy later in this chapter. But for now let me say I consider this the best of both worlds. I'm dollar-cost-averaging my dividends in the more volatile public REITs, while cashing dividend checks (or reinvesting) from my more stable, almost bondlike nontraded REITs. Both REITs are in my long-term growth bucket category, and I intend to hold them for a long time. But they serve two somewhat different purposes: One is more like a bond on steroids, and the other is definitely a stock.

The Lowdown on Loads

A load is a sales charge, and some people get hung up on the fact that a nontraded REIT's load is greater than what you appear to pay for a public REIT. Because of this load, many pundits have advised against nontraded REITs and instead recommended publicly traded REITs. In addition to ignoring the fact that the two have totally separate applications in the *Buckets of Money* strategy, such recommendations are very short-sighted because the load on a private REIT buys a lot more than the salesperson's commission, and the hidden "loads" on public REITs may be far more than you think.

For starters, part of what you're paying for when you buy a nontraded REIT is the cost of due diligence. While most public REITs have seasoned properties and make few acquisitions, nontraded REITs are in acquisition mode, buying billions of dollars of new real estate. In real estate, it's said that you make money when you buy. So upfront due diligence is imperative. Engineering studies, legal reviews, demographic reports, studies of pending legislation—all these and more may need to be done before the REIT makes an offer on a property. While most of these costs are borne by the REIT sponsor, part of any load goes toward this extensive, costly effort. But most of the load costs are the costs of acquiring the capital needed to be a cash or low-leveraged buyer and be able to close escrow quickly while others are trying to arrange financing or raise cash elsewhere.

All of the investor costs are spelled out in the prospectus, and of course one should read that carefully and have a long enough time horizon to invest in an asset class that requires time in order to maximize potential. But remember, if you're spending, say, 10 percent to 12 percent for such costs but getting a property at a 15 percent or 20 percent discount, you're still ahead of the game. That's especially true if there's potential to raise rents in the future, increasing the income and value of the real estate for the eventual liquidity event.

A further, important point: Public REITs have those and other expenses, too. But such costs are not as transparent; they're built into their share price and into their dividend, which is usually 1 percent to 3 percent lower than the nontraded REIT. In fact, studies have shown that when a public REIT with a market capitalization of less than $1 billion raises money by issuing new shares, REIT stock prices typically decline because of dilution of its shares. The lower dividend yield and these costs are, in effect, a "load" levied on a public REIT shareholder. Even with such underwriting, the public REIT is not likely to raise enough cash to compete with the diversification of a multi–billion-dollar nontraded REIT seeking properties it can buy for potentially bargain prices and quick closings.

Instead of seeing load, transparent or otherwise, as some burdensome surcharge, look at it as a positive way to ensure the private REIT will have the capital to put to work and get a good deal for you. What's more, if you buy a REIT that's in an acquisition mode, you don't buy it to sell it right away. You need to hold it long enough to recoup those expenses. Spread out over the length of the time you own the REIT, the load may not amount to much.

There's no real rule of thumb about how big the load might be. And although important, that's not the key issue. More important is finding a REIT that buys the right properties at the right price. Do you like the properties, the credit and quality of the tenants, the dividend the REIT pays? And are you willing to invest your money for a long enough period—at least four to seven years or more—to mitigate the acquisition costs?

When you buy a public REIT, you pay whatever the stock is trading for on that day. In other words, the market sets the share price. Because the private REIT is not traded, its price is based on its capitalized rate, or cap rate, and the overall appetite for real estate in the marketplace. (The cap rate is determined by dividing properties' net operating income by their purchase price.)

The price of a nontraded REIT doesn't usually change until one of two things happen—it becomes a public REIT, in which case underwriters value the stock. Or, it values the shares for compliance reasons (pursuant to Financial Regulatory Authority rules) or for liquidation sometime after all of the funds are raised. But the valuation still doesn't represent what one might get upon a liquidity event.

For instance, if a nontraded REIT goes public, the valuation methodology may be somewhat different. Stocks are typically looked at in terms of price-to-earnings ratio, the price being a multiple of the firm's earnings. A real estate appraisal may not reflect Wall Street's appetite or the amount investors are willing to pay for each dollar of discounted cash flow. Thus, the dividend yield becomes an important component of the stock's ultimate price. And, as stated, dividends from direct ownership in real estate have been historically higher than publicly traded real estate.

To understand how this might work, think of it this way: If you and some partners were purchasing property, the first thing you would do is raise the money needed to buy the real estate, or at least know where to go to get the cash. Next, you find a property you like, do whatever homework you need to do ensure you are getting a good deal, and then buy it. You collect rent, set aside some money for repairs, pay expenses, and then distribute the balance of the cash flow to all of the partners. If you paid, say, $1 million for the property, your financial statement probably would reflect a value of about $1 million. As you raise rents, you get to pocket more cash, but to you the property still feels like it's worth $1 million. After several years, you sell the property for $2 million, and you're feeling pretty good about your *total* return.

You didn't order an appraisal every month to value your real estate in good times and bad. You simply sat on it until there was an appropriate time to sell, a time that allowed you to realize the potential of owning that property. Meanwhile, you collected a decent cash flow each month. So, as is the case with a nontraded REIT, your focus wouldn't be on daily valuations but rather on the cash flow, the security, and eventually the total return.

In short, as I mentioned earlier, buying a nontraded REIT is akin to buying "real" real estate, while buying a public REIT is like buying real estate disguised as a stock. You buy the public REIT based on how the stock market values it. You buy a private REIT based on its capitalized rate of earnings, or cap rate. In other words, a nontraded REIT's price is based more on earnings than emotion.

Are All REITs Low-Leveraged?

No, you have to look for them. Or more likely, get your financial advisor to help you look for them.

Understand a few things about leverage: For starters, it's a good thing in moderation. Most of us know about leverage because that's how we buy our homes. We put down only a fraction of the money, then borrow the rest with a mortgage. That gets us into a house we probably couldn't pay cash for, and it frees up some of our cash for other purposes.

Similarly, a REIT can use leverage to buy more—or more expensive—properties with less cash. More leverage usually means the REIT can pay higher dividends, too. But what's tricky about leverage is that it raises the break-even point. Just as your home mortgage increases your monthly expenses, a REIT raises its fixed costs when it borrows. Instead of, say, a 30 percent occupancy rate being the nonleveraged REIT's break-even point, maybe it's 70 percent with leverage. In a recession, that could make a world of difference.

When you buy a property that has a cap rate higher than your borrowing cost, that's called "positive leverage." For example, if the cap rate on a property is 9 percent and your mortgage is at 7 percent, you're making 2 percent positive leverage. That is, you're actually making money off the money you're borrowing. And that's a good thing and may help to support a higher dividend. Thus, positive leverage—the ability to borrow cheap money to buy cash-flow real estate—can significantly enhance the return on investment.

But too much leverage also can blow up in your face if you are not careful. Most commercial mortgages, for instance, have balloon payments or are relatively short in duration—5, 10, or 15 years. If interest rates are higher when you re-fi the short-term debt, your cash flow could take a hit—along with your REIT's stock price. That's why I prefer low-leverage, nontraded REITs for the growth-and-income portion of your *Buckets of Money* strategy. That way the dividend is based more on the virtues of the underlying real estate and less on the arbitrage between cap rates and loan rates, or supply and demand.

How much leverage, or debt, is okay? You might aim for having 60 percent–70 percent of your REIT money in ones that have no or little debt. "Little debt" might be defined as 20 percent to 40 percent, but any REIT with 50 percent debt, or less, is acceptable. However, it's not just about debt. You also need size for broad diversification— at least $1 billion. You need to be geographically diversified as well as diversified by industry, by tenants, by lease-term maturity, and by different types of property.

What Kinds of Properties Are Best?

Opinions vary on this. Many savvy investors like commercial office buildings that house the headquarters of billion-dollar companies. Another good one is a REIT that leases hotels managed by the major hotel operators. Other popular REITs include those acquiring light industrial, assisted living, upscale apartments, public storage, and boat-storage properties.

The office, multifamily, and industrial sectors are often regarded as prime sectors because either long-term leases are common there or there's such demand that occupancy is high. With other sectors, say hotel and health care, occupancy levels can vary dramatically. But office, multifamily, and industrial tenants tend to be more stable. In fact, with millions of individuals losing their homes to foreclosure, multifamily properties are likely to continue to be in high demand, and financing is much easier in this sector compared to the others. By its nature, the office sector also allows for good diversification among industries because all manner of firms need office space. In addition, the long-term lease signed by a corporate tenant is a legally binding contract. Thus, even a tenant who vacates an office is required by law to pay the agreed-upon rent.

Getting diversified is really important. So let's look in more detail at the possibilities within each sector:

Apartments. Apartment-owning REITs do especially well when the economy is expanding because new jobs lead to the formation of new households. However, this sector is quite sensitive to inflation, which drives up expenses for everything from maintenance to insurance to interest on loans. Further, even if the national economy is doing well, the local or regional economy can be depressed, causing occupancy rates to fall and rents to flatten or decline. Overbuilding also often occurs. So it's especially important for the REIT owner to have several apartment REITs in diverse locations to spread the risk over several geographical areas and management teams, or to own REITs with holdings throughout the country.

Hotels. This is the most economically sensitive of any sector. The highly cyclical industry is prone to overbuilding, and room and occupancy rates can be volatile. Here the keys are location and the operator. While investing in hotels may be aggressive, the sector can nonetheless be worthwhile if you can diversify by investing broadly in a mix of lodging types, such as high-end hotels, inns catering to the business traveler, and those for more budget-minded guests. It's also important to find a REIT that leases to hotels managed by major hotel operators. I doubt that you've ever seen a Marriott or a Hilton boarded up on the side of the road. So having an excellent operator and broad diversification goes a long way toward lowering the risk.

Retail. This sector can include neighborhood shopping centers—usually anchored by a supermarket or a drugstore—as well as regional malls with their trendy, marquee-name stores. Both, of course, depend on the pace of consumer spending. But another variable is the strength of the property market. Strong markets often lead to overbuilding, which lowers rents and depresses operating income. Weak markets, on the other hand, such as we had in 2008–2009, depress the prices of retail centers and thus can offer bargains for REITs with the access to capital to make acquisitions. Though department stores, which anchor the big malls, have been in decline, many mall owners have been adding "entertainment" venues, such as theaters and other special attractions to pull more traffic to the center so that the property is in demand, rents stay high, and shareholder value is enhanced.

A third kind of retail REIT specializes in factory outlets, those out-of-the-way centers at which manufacturers sell to the public at discount prices. This sector has slowed down after a period of rapid growth and represents only a small portion of general merchandise sales. But a well-located outlet center with an excellent tenant base can generate good returns.

Office buildings. Though sometimes prone to overbuilding and fluctuating vacancy rates, the office sector generally is among the most stable because the tenants tend to be long-term. Most of the major pension plans and insurance companies compete for these types of buildings. Chances are a number of the large, beautiful office towers in your city are owned by major institutions or REITs. This sector also provides for good diversification among industries because all kinds of firms need office space. In addition, the long-term lease signed by a corporate tenant is a legally binding contract. Thus, as I mentioned, such a tenant who vacates an office is required by law to pay the agreed-upon rent. Savvy REIT investors particularly favor commercial office buildings in which the tenants are credit-worthy billion-dollar companies renting regional or national headquarters. Or they anchor major buildings with tenants of substantial net worth. Because office properties leased to major tenants tend to be a bit less risky, the dividend yield may not be as high, and the long-term return not as great as for other, more exotic properties.

Long-term leases to Fortune 500–like tenants at fixed rates with annual rent increases tend to act as a cash-flow cushion during economic turndowns and can often be renewed at higher rates upon expiration. Although corporate downsizing in the recent recession hurt this deeply cyclical market, this sector comprises a significant portion of the REIT universe. Investors do need to keep a close eye on potential overbuilding and an even closer eye on the viability and credit-worthiness of the tenant.

Industrial buildings. This sector can include distribution centers, warehouses, light-manufacturing, and research and development facilities. These types of buildings also tend to provide stable returns, in some cases even more stable than returns from office buildings. However, this sector tends to attract both larger and smaller tenants, and sometimes the weaker tenants lack staying power in a weak economic environment. And that can cause a vacancy problem if they struggle financially or eventually go bankrupt.

One of the advantages of industrial buildings is that it doesn't take long to construct and lease these units. That means reaction time is faster than in some other sectors, and therefore there's been less overbuilding. Also when tenants move out, it doesn't take much to prepare the space for the next tenant moving in.

REITs specializing in industrial property can be a good investment especially if management has long-standing relationships with major tenants and concentrates on strong geographical areas.

Health care. These REITs own nursing homes and assisted-living facilities, hospitals, medical office buildings, and rehabilitation centers but typically don't operate them. As a result, overhead is relatively low. Because they don't traditionally receive substantial rent increases, these REITs have had to look largely to consolidation within the industry, acquisitions, and/or mortgage loans to spur cash-flow growth. That means the ability to raise capital either through private equity or reliance on capital markets becomes critical. Investors need to watch out for the financial strength of the lessees, changes in government reimbursement policies, increased regulation, and periodic overbuilding in the assisted-living sector.

The opportunity here is tremendous over the long term. But there are few major players in this sector, so it's important to stick with large, experienced, professionally managed firms with established track records.

Self-storage. Overbuilding plagued this sector for a time, but there's reason to believe self-storage is recession-resistant because in a downturn individuals and businesses cut costs by reducing the space they occupy; that translates into increased need for storage space. Also turning over units from one tenant to the next entails merely sweeping out the unit and re-renting it. So once a self-storage facility is built and occupied, it can be run by on-site managers with limited experience. Mom-and-pop owners dominate the field, meaning lots of opportunities exist for REITs to expand through acquisitions. But because self-storage units are relatively cheap to build and maintain, the supply can easily outpace demand.

Manufactured housing. A far cry from yesterday's mobile-home parks, the manufactured-home community often sports clubhouse, pool, putting greens, and other amenities. Residents normally own the house but lease the land. Because of a low turnover rate, the business is recession resistant, and because the units themselves are maintained by the residents, upkeep costs are low.

Downsides are that it's difficult and time-consuming to get land zoned for manufactured housing, and this type of property can be difficult to finance. However, that also serves to reduce the threat of overbuilding.

Differs from Homes

Sometimes people ask, "Why do I need a REIT? I already own my home, which is a pretty expensive piece of property." Maybe they also have vacation property, apartment houses, or rental homes that they believe give them all the exposure to real estate they'll ever need.

But a REIT, whether private or public, gives a diversification that individual investors can't attain. Owning one, or even several, apartment houses or rental homes does not mean you're diversified. You're probably in one city, or maybe even in one neighborhood in one city. That's dangerous. But a REIT invests in a portfolio of properties, not a single building, and thus the investor automatically gets more diversification.

As for your home, while that may turn out to be a good investment, it doesn't produce current income. Instead, it requires monthly payments and other expenditures.

And a REIT's overall return may be better. A widely-used index of single-family house prices nationwide gained 6.2 percent annually on average from 1976 to 2006. Equity REITs, meanwhile, produced a 7.7 percent compounded annual return and 15.5 percent average annual total return when dividends were reinvested.

Such an attractive total return, plus moderate volatility and a low correlation between REIT returns and house prices, makes home ownership a worthy *complement* to—rather than a substitute for—REIT investing.

The Role of REITs in a Portfolio

REITs, especially nontraded ones, are misunderstood and under-appreciated. Wall Street analysts and many investors have yet to catch on. A case in point: Relatively few 401(k) plans include a REIT option. That spells opportunity. Eventually, REITs may get broader acceptance, and when they do, their value is likely to increase.

Growth in REIT earnings typically comes from higher revenues, lower costs, and new business opportunities. Rents tend to rise as the economy expands. Low occupancy can be increased when skilled owners upgrade buildings and more effectively market them. And aggressive REITs acquire new properties in which the returns outstrip the cost of financing and refurbishment.

In addition to a REIT's growth and income, another huge plus is that REITs add much-needed diversity to your portfolio. They don't move in sync with the stock market. In fact, about 75 percent of the time (though not in the 2008 plunge) public REIT prices move in the opposite direction, giving the investor a nice cushion if the general stock market heads south. And 84 percent of the time public REITs prices trend in an opposite direction from bonds. Adding nontraded REITs further diversifies your portfolio because they are less volatile than stocks and do not correlate in lockstep with public REITs.

A landmark study (see Figure 7.1) by Ibbotson Associates, a leading authority on asset allocation, created sample portfolios of stocks and/or bonds and used various allocations to REITs to measure the effect upon the portfolios' overall return and risk. It concluded that:

- REIT returns were competitive with other types of investments. In fact, REITs' compounded annual returns of 12.5 percent exceeded both government bonds and the Standard & Poor's 500 Index, a common stock-market benchmark.
- Over the last 30 years, the correlation of REIT returns with those of other stocks and bonds has declined appreciably. In other words, the price trend of REITs increasingly goes in an opposite direction from that of stocks and bonds.
- The addition of REIT stocks to a diversified portfolio *raised the portfolio's returns and reduced its risk.* Without REITs, the study said, investors are not earning as high a return as they could for the level of risk they're accepting.
- Adding a 20 percent REIT component to a diversified portfolio maximizes the return and minimizes the risk. Or to put it another way, the diversified portfolio that includes 20 percent real estate earns a better return—*and* has less volatility.

What Should You Look For?

It's important that you diversify when you build a portfolio of REITs. For instance, you don't want to be too concentrated geographically. It wouldn't have been a good idea to have owned property only in, say, Miami or Las Vegas during the recent downturn because those areas were particularly hard hit. Similarly, you want your REITs to be

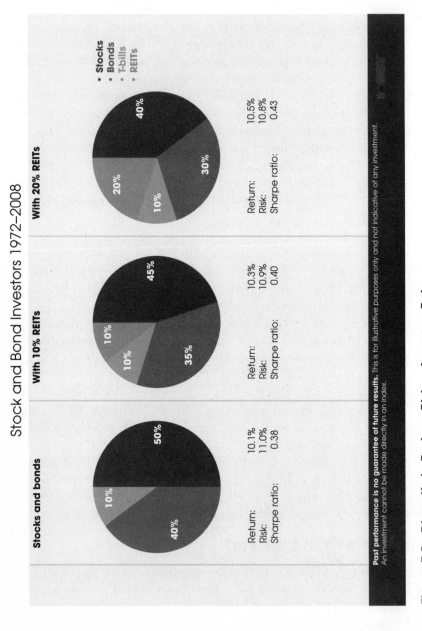

Figure 7.1   Diversify to Reduce Risk or Increase Return

Source: © 2009 Morningstar, Inc. All rights reserved.

spread over several industries. And, in fact, even *within* a particular industry—say, retail—you want a variety of properties.

In addition, look for properties with a range of tenants, but with an emphasis on large, substantial tenants. Further, it would be good to avoid leases that all expire at or near the same time. And avoid REITs that build on "spec," that is, construct a building without first having a commitment from tenants. The days of speculative building are pretty much gone in the commercial marketplace. A shrewd investor wouldn't touch them.

What else should you seek? Look for a management team that can quickly and effectively reinvest capital. It should be able to complete new projects on time and within budget. Also, favor a REIT with properties in which rents are below current market levels. Such properties can provide upside potential as well as downside protection when economic growth slows.

One more caveat: Be careful about chasing yield. Risk and dividends, of course, are related. If you find a REIT that pays 12 percent when most others pay 6 percent, you need to ask: *Why?* Maybe there's an environmental problem or a zoning issue about to come to boil. Or perhaps the yield is being subsidized to attract more money. Look more closely.

Finally, when considering adding a REIT portfolio to your *Buckets of Money* strategy, think globally. Many nontraded REITs have exposure to some of the developed foreign markets. This added level of diversification helps in two ways. First, the obvious: properties located in regions around the world that may be expanding while the United States is contracting. And, second, there may be a currency hedge as well because many times rents are paid in the foreign currency.

Other Questions to Ask

When buying a REIT, also try to find out:

- *What's the long-term demand?* Is this sort of property going to be desirable 5, 10, 20 years from now?
- *Where is the upside?* Rising earnings, of course, is the driving force behind the growth of any company, including REITs. A REIT grows by being able to increase its rents faster than its expenses as well as by making favorable acquisitions and completing profitable new developments.

- *How do I get out and when?* Occasionally, because of overlev- eraging, high price-to-earnings ratios, recession, or a lack of public demand, some big declines have occurred among REIT stocks. More typically, however, the drops have been gradual. Other common stocks seem much more sensitive to negative news. Still, it's a good idea to know at what price you will sell and be prepared to do so. Also, if yours is a non- traded REIT, make sure you have an exit strategy—such as a public listing or sale of the properties. Know how long you are expected to stay in before you can liquidate.

- *What are the cap rates on the properties the REIT is buying?* The cap rate (capitalization rate) means the return expected by the buyer of a property, expressed as a percentage of an all- cash purchase price. Generally, high cap rates indicate lower perceived risk and greater cash flow. Cap rates for apartment REITs, for example, usually range from 7 percent to 9 percent, depending on location, property quality, and supply and demand factors. But due to demand in 2005–2006, cap rates dropped to 5 percent or 6 percent for quality apartments.

  A 10 percent cap property means the REIT will earn 10 percent before REIT expenses on your invested capital. Thus, a $1 million property at a 10 percent cap rate will spin off $100,000 annually. If it were an 8 percent cap, that same property would be valued at $1.25 million because 8 percent of $1.25 million equates to $100,000. Usually, lower cap rates mean a tighter or sellers' market, and higher cap rates typi- cally mean a buyers' market.

  Cap rates fluctuate, depending on market conditions, and should not be the sole deciding factor in buying real estate. But knowing the cap rate of the property in question is a good place to start your evaluation. Buying the above- mentioned apartment at an 8 percent cap rate and selling it at a 6 percent rate would be significantly better than if those numbers were reversed.

Getting Help

Sound complicated? It can be. Every REIT—both traded and nontraded—is unique as far as operating costs, liquidity, divi- dend policies, and so on. So you'll likely need help in evaluating which REITs may be right for you. You'll definitely want proper diversification, and a financial planner can help you with that.

But you also need to be alert. Make sure you grasp the concept. Read the prospectus carefully. Understand that past performance does not guarantee future results. Investments in real estate have certain risks and may be subject to adverse economic and regulatory changes. Nontraded REITs may be illiquid, so be sure to talk to your investment professional about whether investing in real estate is right for you. And public REITs can be exceptionally volatile, so be sure you have a long time-horizon in mind when you buy.

My Personal Bias

I have numerous real estate holdings, brick-and-mortar properties I've acquired over the past 15 years on my own or with partners. I own or have owned self-storage facilities, apartment buildings, office buildings, retail strip centers, condominiums, even gas stations and convenience stores.

I also own five or six nontraded REITs and public REIT stocks and funds. My nontraded REITs consist of low-leveraged commercial office building REITs as well as a globally diversified, multiproperty global REIT and a multifamily REIT. I tend to favor the nontraded REITs because they are similar to the real estate I already own. I feel the REIT properties have been acquired at reasonable cap rates (7 percent to 10 percent), and the share price doesn't reflect the ups and downs of the stock market. I like that.

I also feel that a low or moderately leveraged nontraded REIT in Bucket 3A can act as a buffer between the relatively "safe" money I have in Buckets 1, 2, and the long-term growth money in my Bucket 3B. I don't have concerns about interest rates changing the value of my investment, and the yield I get from REITs (6 percent to 7 percent) is better than any high-quality or even medium-quality bond.

My nontraded REITs are destined to go public someday, or, I hope, liquidate at an appreciated value. Then I look forward to some possible capital gains, though that's certainly not guaranteed. In all cases, the tenants are paying for all of the expenses ("triple net" leases), and there are annual, contractual rent increases on all of the leases.

On the public REIT side, my REIT funds in Bucket 3B give me broad diversification with low expenses and liquidity if I ever need to get my hands on some of my REIT money. Although the share price fluctuates daily, I am effectively diversifying my stock portfolio by adding real estate.

Because I have a significant sum of personally-owned real estate in my taxable account, I have acquired my REITs through my IRA and other retirement accounts. Thus, I'm not getting the advantage of tax deferral through depreciation. But that's okay because I don't have to report the taxable portion of the dividend, either.

I'm sometimes asked to describe the upside on my REITs in comparison to the upside on my other real estate holdings. The upside is evident on real estate with mortgages of 60 percent to 80 percent of the value. If I put $300,000 down on a $1 million property and earn income of $21,000 per year, I have a 7 percent yield. If the property appreciates 5 percent, then my total return is approximately 24 percent ($21,000 yield plus $50,000 appreciation = $71,000, or 24 percent of my $300,000 investment).

If I put $300,000 into a 7 percent–yielding, all-cash REIT that appreciates 5 percent, my return is only 12 percent (7 percent plus 5 percent). So with leverage I dramatically increase my potential for capital gain. Thus, owning brick-and-mortar real estate in my personal accounts (versus my IRA) makes sense. My REITs are considered long-term retirement vehicles. With low leverage comes lower tax benefits and lower risk. Therefore, I feel it's quite appropriate for me to own REITs in my retirement account. However, an individual with substantial personal holdings might be well suited to invest some of that personal money in REITs and take advantage of depreciation and long-term capital gains tax treatment upon sale.

Even though a significant amount of my total net worth is tied up in real estate, I am still striving to achieve a 20 percent to 30 percent allocation to REITs in my investment portfolio. The reason is simple. All my nontraded REITs may give me stock market–like returns with bond market–like (or better) yields. So I'm earning 6 percent to 7 percent to wait for my properties to either be sold (at, it's hoped, a profit for which shareholders are entitled to 90 percent in a REIT) or listed as an IPO on the New York Stock Exchange. While I could take the income if I needed it, I'm currently reinvesting all of my dividends, dollar-cost averaging with every quarterly check.

If my nontraded REITs do list, there's a decent chance they may list at a higher price than I paid for them. Why? Let's say the properties were bought with an average cap rate of 7 percent to 8 percent. That means for every dollar I expect a return of seven to eight cents per year. Public REITs usually trade with a price/ earnings ratio of 15 to 20 and a dividend yield of about 5 percent. If a 5 percent dividend produces a 15 PE when my 7 percent or 8 percent REIT goes public, it could garner a 10 percent to 20 percent or larger premium. In other words, for my REIT to pay out a yield commensurate with the public REIT marketplace, Wall Street would need to value my REIT a little bit higher so my 7 percent to 8 percent yield on the nontraded REIT translates into a 5 percent yield in the public marketplace, assuming my REITs are priced to the market. At least that's what I hope for.

Now there's certainly no guarantee this will happen, but it is a clear possibility. Even if my nontraded REIT goes public some day at the exact same share price as I paid for it (in other words, no real estate appreciation or higher income), I will have been paid 7 percent to 8 percent cash flow to wait. I consider that an excellent complement to my Bucket 3B long-term growth account.

Whether you choose the upside potential and the volatility of a public REIT, the potentially higher dividend yield and lesser liquidity of a nontraded REIT, or a combination of the two, understand that the real estate world is constantly changing. Finding the right REIT or REITs, placing them in the right account (taxable or tax-deferred), spending your dividend or reinvesting, leveraging or not leveraging—all these are decisions to be made as part of your *Buckets of Money* strategy and are best made with the help of a Certified Financial Planner (CFP), CPA, and tax attorney.

Remember, practically everyone can benefit from an investment in REITs. Matching the right REIT with your goals, objectives, time horizon, and risk tolerance will be the key to a successful investment in real estate.

A Final Word

A broad range of investors, from huge pension funds to individual retired school teachers, use REITs to help them achieve their investment goals. Maybe you're a retiree seeking to fatten your income stream while protecting yourself from the ravages of inflation.

Or perhaps you're an active stock and bond investor concerned about the volatility of a concentrated portfolio. In either case, REITs offer an efficient way to solve an age-old investment problem: How can I increase my return without taking on more overall risk?

Diversifying your portfolio with real estate is one of the best ways to manage the ups and downs of the financial markets. With REITs, you not only get dividends now that can cushion a downturn, but you also get prospects for moderate future growth from a tangible, hard asset—and you don't need to be a landlord to participate.

As I said, you should regard REITs as a complement, not a substitute, for stocks and bonds. The long-term returns of REITs stocks are likely to be somewhat less than the returns of high-growth stocks and somewhat more than the returns of bonds. Most REITs have a small-to-medium equity market capitalization, and thus their returns may be comparable to other small- or mid-sized companies.

As to the choice between public or nontraded REITs, you might think of it this way: Buyers of public REITs are diversifying their stock portfolio, while buyers of nontraded REITs are diversifying their money. Perhaps the best of all worlds is to do both.

CHAPTER

8

Play It Smart When It Comes to Personally Owned Real Estate

Most of us own one home, and if we are blessed, maybe we have a second one as a vacation retreat. Many folks have watched their homes appreciate over time, and thus they have a bias toward personally owned real estate. But that, of course, begs the question: Is a home or vacation retreat a good investment? If so, where does it fit as part of your retirement plan? And should you buy more personally owned real estate as a way of expanding your wealth in retirement?

Real estate can be attractive for numerous reasons. One reason, of course, is that it includes land, which is in limited supply. Usually that land also includes buildings that cost more each year to build or replace. As the cost of construction increases, so does the value of well-maintained buildings. In addition, real estate has gotten hammered over the past two or three years, so bargains abound for someone with enough savvy and cash or financing.

This chapter will discuss topics one rarely finds in financial books: first, options for dealing with your current home, from refinancing to paying off the mortgage to taking out a reverse mortgage. Then we'll consider whether acquiring additional property is a viable way to add to your long-term retirement assets.

Your Home and Your Future

Is owning the home you live in your best investment? Or would it be smarter to rent? To make that determination one must place an

economic value on some of the ancillary and/or emotional benefits of home ownership. For example, in my case, when Jeanne and
I were younger and raising our children, we weren't concerned with
the investment aspects of our home as much as we wanted to have a
house that was big enough to accommodate our four children. We
also needed one that our kids could invite their friends to. That way
we could keep tabs on our kids and get to know their friends. From
that standpoint, our home was, by far, our best investment regardless of the economics.

Is It Affordable?

Beyond the emotional value placed on home ownership one must
also be sure whatever home purchased is affordable now and in the
future. It's foolish to buy a home at any and all costs. Ask anyone
who used subprime financing or overpaid for their home and is
now facing a short sale or foreclosure. For them, their home was
probably their worst investment. But assuming you have an ade-
quate down payment and can obtain financing at a reasonable cost,
let's explore a home as an investment in the hypothetical below.

Paying rent to someone else is a drag. So let's say you decide
to buy a home instead. You go to your financial advisor and ask
him how much of a mortgage you can afford based on your combined hypothetical $100,000 per year income. He quickly says
between $2,000 and $3,000 per month. He also tells you that at
6.5 percent interest that amounts to a maximum loan of about
$300,000 to $400,000. You have $50,000 in the bank set aside for
a down payment. Being conservative, you feel comfortable with a
$350,000 purchase. You ask what will be your approximate monthly
"all-in" cost? Your advisor writes something along these lines
(which will vary depending on property taxes, maintenance, and
the like):

$300,000 Loan @ 6.5 percent	$1,900/month
Property taxes	$ 300/month
Insurance	$ 50/month
Maintenance, utilities, and upkeep	$ 250/month
TOTAL	**$2,500/month**

You compare that to the $1,650 per month you are paying in rent and ask if this is a good deal or not. Your advisor reminds you about the tax benefits of home ownership (mortgage interest and property taxes are deductible expenses), so you do a side-by-side comparison:

RENT (per month)	OWN (per month)		NET COST AFTER TAXES (25 percent tax bracket)
$1,650	Mortgage	$1,900	$1,500
	Property tax	$ 300	$ 225
	Insurance	$ 50	$ 50
	Maintenance, etc.	$ 250	$ 250
TOTAL $1,650		**$2,500**	**$2,025**

So you can see the actual cost to own the hypothetical home is $375 per month more than renting. That doesn't sound too bad since you locked into a 30-year fixed-rate loan that won't increase the way rent does and you will be paying down some principal on the loan each year, building equity as you go. Also, with some luck, houses will go up in value in the future.

So let's do the math. In 10 years you will have paid your $300,000 loan down to $254,000. So you will have built up $46,000 of equity plus your $50,000 down payment. If the property appreciates at only 2.5 percent per year in 10 years, your $350,000 property will be worth about $450,000. If you then sold after, say, $30,000 in selling costs, you'd net $420,000, pay off your $254,000 loan and walk away with $166,000.

Keep in mind that you invested $50,000 in a down payment and you spent $375 per month in costs beyond the cost of renting (assuming the rents and the extra costs never went up). That's about a 7 percent return on your money. Not exceptional, but it's tax-free because this was a primary residence and the gain upon sale was less than $500,000 (a married couple's capital-gains exemption). Furthermore, it's not realistic to assume rents wouldn't have gone up over 10 years, so your real tax-free return could be closer to 8 percent or 9 percent. Again, that's assuming only a 2.5 percent annual price appreciation. Of course, it's also not realistic to assume you won't have to spend some cash on upkeep and maintenance beyond normal wear and tear on your home.

So where does that leave us? An affordable home as a principal residence like the one in this example isn't a bad investment by any means but probably—we hope—not the best one you'll ever make. The key, then, is buying an *affordable* home, not buying one you like but really can't afford.

However, while personal real estate can be a decent investment, it rarely beats the returns of the stock market. Real estate should be an important component in everyone's portfolio but not the *only* component. Nonetheless your home is an investment, and as with all your investments, you should carefully consider your risk tolerance and time horizon before investing. And doing these types of calculations can really help.

Risk Awareness

You should be cognizant of all of the risks associated with home ownership. In 2006 and 2007, the real estate market began to unravel due mostly to overly aggressive buyers of real estate working with overly aggressive mortgage brokers, greedy banks, and subprime lenders. Real estate speculators went on a buying frenzy, overpaying billions of dollars for just about any house, co-op, condo, or high-rise condo they could get their hands on. Teaser interest rates were low. Negative-amortization loans were common, and piggyback first- and second-trust deeds for more than 100 percent of the property's value didn't seem to bother people. That's because 10 percent to 20 percent annual appreciation meant that even if you were in a negative cash-flow situation, you could always sell your house a year or two later for significantly more than you paid.

As with tulips and tech stocks, a housing crash was sooner or later bound to happen. The real estate market imploded, property values dropped, and teaser interest rates reset at higher levels. Individuals who bought over their heads or speculated based on unrealistic future real estate prices got hammered. For them, real estate was an albatross, not an investment.

Real estate, like stocks, is a long-term investment. Short-term speculation in any investment is very risky and dangerous.

However, I do feel for the inexperienced first-time homebuyers who didn't know any better and were taken advantage of. Losing your home is a tough lesson to learn. However, if these individuals lied about their income, as many did, just to jump on the housing bandwagon, perhaps they too are getting what they deserve.

Unfortunately, some of them were bamboozled by unscrupulous lenders just wanting to make a loan or two and by overzealous realtors that wanted to sell a home at any cost. Now many of them owe more than the house is worth and, worse yet, can't afford to make their house payments, which are likely to be as much as two times greater than they were a year or two ago when the house was first bought. If the house goes into foreclosure, their credit will be ruined for many years to come. That means their borrowing costs on just about everything will be higher. For these individuals, their home is hardly a good investment at all.

Having said all of that, I'm sure there are many, many high-quality real estate and mortgage professionals who do tell the truth. They will tell you that for most of us owning a home makes a lot of sense. Obviously, you must live somewhere so owning, as long as it's at a reasonable price and in your affordability range, is probably the right thing to do. What's an affordable range? The general guideline for how much house you can afford is to take your gross monthly income and divide by three. Your mortgage payment, taxes, and insurance should not exceed that amount. Also, all recurring debts—including your potential mortgage payment, taxes and insurance, credit cards, car loans, and the like—should not exceed 40 percent of your gross income. Thus, if you and your spouse earn $100,000 combined gross income, you should not have annual debt payments exceeding $40,000 per year, including no more than $33,000 for the principal, and interest on your home mortgage, taxes, and insurance.

Making the Most of Equity

Even after the recent plunge in home values, many Americans have an enormous buildup of equity in their homes. In fact, that equity is likely one of their largest assets, especially if the mortgage has been paid down over the years or even paid off. That home equity can be a valuable source of extra income during retirement *if* you can figure out a way to unlock that property's value.

That's what people do, for instance, when they take out a home-equity loan or a home-equity line of credit. Those are harder to get now. What's more, many seniors don't qualify because of low income. And in any case, even when such credit was readily available, it meant taking on more debt, which is generally not what you want to do as a retiree or near-retiree.

So let's look at some of the other options.

Trading Down.   If your home is larger than you require, moving to a smaller place or to a less expensive area may be a good way to increase your retirement income. (The tax laws encourage this: You can generally exclude up to $250,000 of the profit—$500,000 if you're married—on the sale of your principal residence from capital-gains tax if you've lived in the home two years out of the last five.) The difference between what you sell your old house for and what you pay for the new one can give a sharp boost to your retirement nest egg. Of course, you'll need to factor closing costs and moving expenses into that equation as well.

A smaller home—or one in a less expensive area—usually means lower real estate taxes and perhaps smaller bills for heating, cooling, insurance, and maintenance. If your move is from a single-family house to a condominium, your costs will be reduced even more because outside painting, roof repair, landscaping, and similar costs will be covered by your condo fees.

But consider the disadvantages: You'll likely have less space and maybe a less attractive house. Besides, a lot of folks want to stay in their family home near their familiar haunts and among their closest associates. Even if you have a lot of equity tied up in the house, you may not want to move because you love the home and the neighborhood. So, increasingly, people seek other ways to eliminate or reduce the mortgage burden.

Pay Off Your Mortgage.   It used to be that by the time most people retired they'd paid off their mortgage and could count on the equity in their home to help support them after they stopped working or to help pay for nursing-home costs later in life.

That's no longer true. In 1992, 18 percent of Americans aged 65 to 74 had housing debt, according to numbers compiled by the Employee Benefit Research Institute. But by 2007, that percentage had risen to 43 percent.

Since then, the amount of home equity has declined for many homeowners. So for those nearing retirement, it's important to be conservative when it comes to protecting your home equity. Thus, all things being equal, it might be better to pay down or pay off your mortgage than carry it into retirement. But all things are rarely equal.

And, of course, for some retirees, paying down the mortgage isn't an option. But if you have savings beyond what's needed for living expenses, is it ever a good idea to hold onto a mortgage in retirement instead of using that money to pay it down?

The answer is: *Maybe.* Let's look at the advantages of paying off the mortgage.

For starters, you'll get a better return on your money than with other risk-free assets, such as bank CDs, Treasury bills and bonds, and money-market accounts. It's easy to see how getting rid of a 6 percent mortgage gives you a bigger bang for your buck than receiving 2 percent interest on a CD. If you have a stock portfolio, you might earn a high enough return to come out ahead of a mortgage but, of course, as recent years have shown only too clearly, stocks can lose money, too.

What's more, paying off your mortgage will reduce the interest you pay over the term of the loan by thousands, maybe tens of thousands, of dollars. Paying extra or paying off early also allows some borrowers to avoid paying private mortgage insurance. Paying off the loan is especially attractive for some homeowners with small loans who pay an amount of interest that doesn't exceed the standard IRS deduction for the nonitemizing taxpayer.

Having no mortgage to pay would be a wonderful bonus should a calamity—such as a major health issue or a severe financial setback—occur. Mortgage debt can be particularly insidious when home prices plummet as they have recently. Not having a mortgage means you're no longer concerned about owing a debt that's greater than the worth of the house.

If you're about to send a kid to college, taking money out of your savings and using it to prepay your mortgage may reduce the assets that are counted against you when applying for college financial aid. And, of course, there's a psychic reward that comes with not having to send in that check every month. Just dreaming about what you could do with all those extra bucks might be itself worth the price of admission.

So paying off the mortgage, or paying it down, may be for *most* people a sound financial goal. But whether it is for *you* depends largely on how much other money you have and what pressing needs you have for it.

A Fan of Flexibility

Me, I'm a fan of financial flexibility. I wouldn't rush to pay off the mortgage just because I could. (And one in five seniors has a mortgage and the dough to pay it down by selling some of their other investments, according to the Boston College Center for Retirement Research.) Even if I had the money to eliminate the mortgage, I'd want to think through the ramifications of keeping that debt.

For instance, don't even *consider* prepaying your mortgage if you have significant credit-card debt. Interest rates on your plastic are at least a couple times that of your mortgage. Further, that interest— unlike the interest paid on your mortgage—is not tax deductible. So get your credit-card debt under control first. In addition, make sure you've got an emergency fund. That means hoarding enough cash to cover your expenses for at least a few months in case you lose your job, are injured, or suffer some other unexpected financial blow.

Plus, don't forget about your need for money in retirement. Owning your home free and clear won't be very comforting if you can't afford to put food on the table. So before you allocate a large sum toward your mortgage, be certain you've taken full advantage of tax-favored retirement plans, such as your 401(k)s or an IRA. And make sure you have enough life insurance to cover the mortgage, living expenses, and education costs. Even if you don't have others depending on you, disability insurance or long-term-care insurance might be good ideas, too.

Explore what will happen to your taxes if you pay down or pay off your mortgage and thus reduce or eliminate your mortgage-interest deduction. Depending on what else is going on in your financial life, doing so could end up increasing what you owe the government.

And, finally, be sure to check your mortgage contract for details that could hurt you. For example, some lenders penalize you if your prepayment exceeds a certain amount (say, 20 percent a year) or if it occurs within a certain period (such as in the first five years of the loan).

Making a decision to prepay your mortgage is more complicated than it may appear on the surface. Before you do what may feel good emotionally, be sure you've thought it all through. I recommend you talk to a financial and/or tax professional before making the final call.

Pay Your Mortgage from a Roth.   If you're able to save enough to send in extra mortgage payments and pay down your loan, maybe you could put that money to work in a smarter way—such as a Roth IRA. If you were able to wisely invest that Roth money, you might get a better return than you would from prepaying a mortgage of 6 percent or 7 percent. Keep in mind that mortgage interest is tax deductible, and a Roth accumulates its earnings tax-deferred.

So let's say you're in a combined federal-state 33 percent tax bracket. A deductible 6 percent mortgage would effectively cost you, say, 4 percent. So anything you earned in your Roth IRA above 4 percent would be gravy.

Further, if you decide you're ready to be mortgage-free, and if you qualify, you might withdraw money from the Roth to either pay off the mortgage balance in full or simply withdraw enough money to cover the mortgage payments. The latter approach would allow you to keep your mortgage-interest deduction *and* use the Roth money tax-free.

Yes, you'd need to start on this plan early enough to build up a sufficient balance in your Roth. (Remember, the current maximum yearly contribution is $5,000, or $6,000 if you're age 50 or more.) And you'd still need to write that check each month to the lender. But if you knew the tax-free source from which the money was coming—*and* you kept what's likely your biggest tax deduction—maybe it would be worth it.

Refinancing.   Lower mortgage rates are good and can save you money, especially if you have an adjustable-rate mortgage that's due to reset to a higher rate. But refinancing isn't the slam dunk it once seemed. Getting a new loan is harder than it used to be because your income and credit score are checked far more carefully. Further, not only are home prices not rising as they did just a few years ago, they've fallen sharply in many areas, meaning you have less equity in the home.

Plus, even if you can get a loan, you want to be quite sure the deal makes sense financially. In other words, don't be drawn in by the lower rate alone.

When deciding whether to refinance your mortgage, you also want to look realistically at how long you plan to stay in the home. Closing costs usually total several thousand dollars, so it's important figure how long it would take you to break even. For example, let's say home-mortgage rates have fallen to where you can refinance at a 2 percent lower interest rate and that will reduce your monthly payment by $200.

But, say, your closing costs are $6,000. Even if those costs are rolled into the new loan amount instead of being paid out of pocket, you're still looking at 30 months before you'd break even on your refinancing. So if there's a chance you'll be moving in less than 2½ years, the refinance may actually cost you.

Another thing that many people forget is that refinancing also extends the term of the loan. If you've been making payments on your 30-year fixed mortgage for 15 years, you only had another 15 to go. If you refinance for another 30-year mortgage, you can get a lower monthly payment but you may well have more total interest expense over the years because you've extended the term.

So what some people do is refinance from a 30-year to a 15-year mortgage. But, of course, choosing a shorter term means a higher monthly payment. So you need to calculate if changing the terms makes financial sense.

Another tactic for those who are retired, or are about to retire, is to refinance—not necessarily to lock in lower rates—but to re-amortize the loan. For instance, if 15 years remain on your loan, refinancing to a 30-year loan could cut your payments substantially and, thus, increase your disposable income.

When you die, you'd be leaving your children a home with a loan outstanding. But is it really important to leave them a house that's paid off versus leaving them, say, an $800,000 home with a $200,000 mortgage? Meanwhile, you would have freed up cash flow to improve your standard of living. Keep in mind that interest on refinancing or home-equity loans is deductible as home-mortgage interest (versus investment interest) only on principal amounts of

$100,000 beyond your acquisition debt—that is, the amount of the loan before you refinanced.

Take Out a Reverse Mortgage.   Retirees whose nest eggs were scrambled in 2007–2008 increasingly are turning to reverse mortgages to help them fund a comfortable lifestyle in their later years. The number of federally insured reverse mortgages hit 112,015 in 2008, up from about 43,000 in 2005, according to federal housing data. Such borrowers are looking for cash, but don't want to draw down already depleted investment accounts.

And that can work—but at a risk. Using a reverse mortgage to finance the "good life" can result in consuming much, if not all, of your home equity. If you want to take a dream vacation or get cash to invest, a reverse mortgage is a bad idea. That's because if you need cash for future needs, such as long-term care or medical major expenses, you could find yourself out of options. What's more, these loans are very expensive and the amount you owe grows every month.

Reverse mortgages were once largely the last resort for impoverished oldsters who had no other income. But this kind of mortgage has become so popular because it allows seniors to turn their home equity into tax-free cash. With a reverse mortgage, you can increase your income and continue to live in your present home for life. Many homeowners get interested in reverse mortgages so they can stay in their own homes. But perhaps the best way to evaluate a reverse mortgage is to compare it to what you'd get by selling your home and using the proceeds to buy or rent a new place.

How It Works.   It's called a *reverse* mortgage because the principal balance gets larger, not smaller, over time, and because the bank pays you; you don't pay the bank. Only homeowners age 62 or older can take out a reverse mortgage. The younger you are when you take out a reverse mortgage, the more the compound interest will grow—and thus, the more you'll owe. Generally, the older you are, the more your home is worth, and the lower interest rates are, the more cash you can get. (Many seniors don't qualify for home-equity loans or home-equity lines of credit because of low income. And in any case, such loans require a monthly repayment, so they don't solve cash-flow problems.)

A reverse mortgage generally must be a "first" mortgage, meaning it must be the primary debt against your home. So if you already have a mortgage, you generally must either pay it off *before* you get the reverse mortgage or pay it off *with* the money you get from the reverse mortgage.

The interest on a reverse mortgage accrues, and the loan doesn't need to be repaid until the borrower dies or moves out of the home. In the 1970s and 1980s, some questionable reverse-mortgage programs resulted in owners being put out of their houses when the size of the debt exceeded the value of the property. But government safeguards now ensure homeowners will never owe more than the home's value. That's because if the value of the house falls below the loan amount, the lender absorbs the difference.

The money can be used for any purpose, and the proceeds can usually come in the form of a monthly check, a lump sum, a line of credit, or some combination of these. The payout doesn't affect your Social Security payments. And you don't need to repay the loan as long as you live in the home. (The loan is usually repaid from the proceeds from the sale of the house after you move or die.)

The size of the loan depends in part on the specific reverse-mortgage program you select and also on the kind of cash advances you choose. Most homeowners qualify for the biggest cash advances under the U.S. government's home-equity conversion mortgage (HECM) program, which is backed by the Federal Housing Administration (see www.hud.gov). The FHA tells HECM lenders how much they can lend you, based on your age and your home's value. The HECM limits your loan costs, and though HECMs usually are less expensive than privately insured reverse mortgages, they can still be costly. Generally, figure on getting access to no more than about 30 percent to 50 percent of the equity in your house because lenders don't want to be left holding the bag if house values plummet. But if the market value of your home is well above the average house price in your area, you might be able to get a larger loan from a private lender.

Ideally, you want the biggest loan at the lowest cost. But the two don't always go hand in hand, and their complex features can sometimes make them difficult to evaluate. For help in figuring out the best terms, talk to your financial advisor. You may also want to

check out AARP's Reverse Mortgage Education Project (www.aarp
.org/money/revmort).

Reverse mortgages can be an expensive way to generate income
compared to, say, trading down to a smaller home. Loan fees and
closing costs are higher than for traditional mortgages, often
running into the five figures. However, these may be wrapped
into the loan amount, meaning that there's little upfront cost.
Because the loan is payable at death, heirs may feel shortchanged,
although they can take out a conventional mortgage to pay off the
reverse mortgage.

Reverse mortgages make the most sense if you're looking for an
ongoing source of income through retirement or you need a large
lump sum. It doesn't make much sense if you might move in a few
years or just need cash for some relatively small bills. That's because
the stiff up-front expenses—such as origination fees, closing costs,
and mortgage insurance—can drive the effective short-term loan
rate skyward.

Also, note that a reverse mortgage doesn't reduce your housing costs unless it's used to pay off your existing mortgage. With a
reverse mortgage, you remain the owner of your home and are still
responsible for paying property taxes and homeowners insurance,
and for making property repairs.

While the payouts are tax-free, the accrued loan interest isn't
deductible until or if the borrower starts paying off the loan. Each
payment that you receive from the lender reduces your home
equity—and increases the amount of principal and interest that you
owe on the mortgage. This means that the owner will net less when
the home is eventually sold, unless the value of the home appreciates more rapidly than the rise in the reverse-mortgage balance.

On the other hand, if you face a serious retirement-income
shortage, this reduction in equity—really a lessening of your heirs'
potential inheritance—may be better than lowering your standard of living. So for an increasing number of retirees, adding to
their cash flow trumps the downsides of reverse mortgages. It can
be especially helpful in the early years of retirement when you
can travel and get out more.

But remember, the more of your equity you use now, the less
you will have later when you may need it more. If you're not
facing a financial emergency now, consider postponing a reverse
mortgage.

Finally, another word of caution: Be disciplined about how you use any retirement windfall, whether it's from a reverse mortgage or from some other equity-tapping technique. The Securities and Exchange Commission has come out strongly against individuals borrowing against their homes to buy investments such as stocks, and the commission is especially critical of borrowing to buy variable annuities.

Get an Unofficial Reverse Mortgage. If you're put off by the fees involved and/or the administrative hassle of applying for a reverse mortgage, perhaps you could cut a deal with your kids. Tell them the house will eventually be theirs but meanwhile, you need more cash flow to live a comfortable retirement lifestyle. Maybe they could take over some or all of the mortgage payments and provide you with the additional income you need. They could even charge you an interest rate below that of a traditional reverse mortgage. So, your kids would be creating a low-cost reverse mortgage for you.

A trust deed can protect the repayment of the loan plus interest before the balance is distributed to the heirs. The kids will be paid back after you die when they sell the house. My strong suggestion would be to get any such agreement in writing. Reach a clear understanding of who gets what and when. In fact, just to be safe, it would be a good idea to hire a real estate attorney to go over your agreement.

Think It Through

Another suggestion: Take your time and think carefully through any plan to tap into your home equity. After all, it has taken many years to build up that value. Whether you're trading down to a smaller, less expensive home; paying off or paying down the current loan; refinancing or re-amortizing; or taking out an official or unofficial reverse mortgage, don't act in haste. Take the time to unlock that value in the smartest way.

Most people already have a fair amount of real estate if one considers the family home. Is that a Buckets-like investment? It *could* be, but probably you shouldn't look at it that way. After all, unlike your stocks and income property, you can't exactly sell it and live off it in retirement—you'll still need a place to live. So the fact that your home appreciated may not mean too much if when you sell it, you have to buy another, equally expensive home.

So it's best not to count on your home as part of your Buckets strategy. However, when you ultimately sell, your home equity can be a great place to find some cash for immediate or deferred income.

If your home turns out to be a great investment, that's a plus. But if it doesn't, you've still planned well and will be okay. And, understand, the house may not turn out to be a great investment because it (1) may not rise in value (2) may rise but you may not be able to sell it for what it's worth when you want to, and (3) you may need to buy another one, which could end up costing you as much, or more.

The best plan, then, is to just live in your house and enjoy it. If the home eventually helps fund your retirement, that's a windfall . . . but not something you're counting on.

Buying Other Real Estate

It's not just the lenders and mortgage brokers who were to blame for the mortgage meltdown in 2007–2008. You and I also can share in the guilt. We were all born with a greed chromosome. We all want to make a quick buck, and we all probably know someone who has done so in real estate. When a friend or relative makes a killing on a real estate investment and we're sitting in cash, it roils that greed chromosome and the jealousy one, too. If Charlie can get rich with real estate, so can *I*!

The Fantasy

Or we attend a seminar where someone ridicules you because you're not using your home's "idle equity." You hear this pitch: "Borrow the max out of your home and then redeploy that money into more real estate, or into the stock market or a life insurance policy or annuity. And when your home goes up in value, borrow some more!" You've seen the late-night infomercials and have probably read columns and books by people recounting how they made a killing by leveraging themselves to the hilt and buying income property.

This is fantasy for most of us. Just because someone else got lucky doesn't mean you will. I have little sympathy for experienced adults who have gotten themselves into this mess in an attempt to time the real estate market using little or no money down and short-term teaser rates. They expect to buy while real estate is going up in a frenzy and expect to sell it at the top to some poor sucker just before it crashes. They care little about the economics of the deal. These people aren't investors but gamblers.

Like stocks, real estate can not only grow in value over the long term but also produce income. And it's usually not as volatile as stocks because it takes a lot longer to buy or sell property than just calling up your mutual fund or broker. So there's less day-to-day fluctuation in prices, and that's good.

But on the other hand, this lack of liquidity also means you can get stuck with an unsalable piece of property on which you're paying a mortgage, taxes, and upkeep, and that's not so great. So real estate, while often a good choice for your long-term buckets, is better as a complement to stocks rather than as a replacement for them.

Keep in mind also that buying rental property usually requires a large initial cash outlay as well as what's often lots of management hassles for you, the landlord. And, ideally, you'll want to diversify, meaning multiple properties—and that can really get costly.

Single-Family Rentals?

One thing I'm asked all the time is, "Should we sell our home or keep it and rent it out?" I must admit I'm not a huge fan of buying single-family homes as rental property. That's because if your tenant moves out you now have a 100 percent vacancy rate. I much prefer multifamily units or light industrial properties with several tenants. That way, one tenant moving out will have a smaller impact on your cash flow. Also, if you have, say, 30 units and you raise the rent $20 per month, your income just grew by $600 a month. That not only adds $7,200 per year to the bottom line, it probably adds $100,000 in value to the property were you to sell.

Nonetheless, many real estate investors have done very well owning single-family homes as rentals. It certainly can work if you have the talent; temperament and skills to be a landlord; enough cash in the bank to carry you through the tough times; and a Rolodex of competent and trustworthy repairmen, painters, gardeners, and electricians. Converting your principal residence, however, into a rental property may be ill-advised. That's because after three years pass from the time you move out of your principal residence, you give up any hope of selling the house and receiving up to $500,000 of your capital gain ($250,000 if you're single) tax-free unless you move back into the home as a principal residence for two years.

Tax-free capital gains upon sale is one of the great tax advantages of home ownership. Generally speaking, if you live in your home as a principal residence for at least 24 months out of the 60 months prior to sale, you can sell your home and exclude any capital-gains taxes (subject to the limitations mentioned above). However, a new rule, effective in 2009, limits how much you can exclude from capital-gains taxation if the principal residence you're selling formerly was owned by you as a rental, vacation home, or other nonprimary residence. You must pro rate the gain, depending on how long you owned the property before making it your personal residence.

For example, let's assume you paid $100,000 in 2004 for a house that you didn't use for your primary residence. Maybe it was a rental, a vacation home, or just a second home; that doesn't matter. The key is that it was *not* your primary residence. In January 2012 you move into this home and make it your primary residence and live there for at least two years. Then in January 2014 you move out and sell it for $250,000, which creates $150,000 of gain.

Because you've lived in it for more than two years of the last five, you do qualify for the exclusion of up to $250,000 ($500,000 married couple) for a personal residence. However, since you didn't use it as a primary residence for the entire time of ownership, part of the gain will not qualify as "primary residence gain."

To determine how much of the gain you can use as primary residence gain, you must figure the number of months you lived in it divided by the total ownership months after 2008. So if it was sold in January 2014, you lived in the home for 24 months and owned it for 60 months. That means that 40 percent (24 divided by 60) of the gain on the home is primary residence gain. In this example, the gain is $150,000 so $60,000 ($150,000 × .40) can be excluded; the other $90,000 is taxable.

Another confusing part of this new rule is the ownership period can extend past five years. To qualify as a primary residence, you must live in a place you own for at least 24 of the past 60 months (two out of five years). But the proration of gain is not limited to five years. If you own a property for more than five years after 2008, the percentage you can exclude can be a relatively small amount.

For instance, let's change the facts of the last example: Instead of moving in January 2012, you make the house your primary residence in January 2015. Then after two years, you decide to sell (sale price is $300,000, for a gain of $200,000). Part of the gain will be primary residence gain because you did live there for at least 24 months of the 60 months prior to sale. But now you have owned it for 8 years (after 2008) but only lived in it for two. Given those facts, 25 percent (24 months divided by 96 months) of the gain can be excluded, or $50,000.

However, the *most* confusing part of this new law is that any time after the house was your primary residence is not counted as part of the equation. Only monthly ownership (after 2008) prior to primary residence use is used to determine how much of the gain can be excluded. Got that?

Further Disadvantages

Other disadvantages exist when you convert your principal home into a rental property. For example, when you own residential real estate, you get to depreciate the cost-basis of the building structure (not the land) over 27.5 years. Thus, if your original cost-basis for the structure plus capital improvements of the building itself cost, say, $275,000, you get a $10,000 depreciation write off each year for the next 27.5 years. That could save someone in the 25 percent tax bracket about $2,500 per year in taxes.

If you bought your home years ago, the cost-basis likely is quite low and the capital gain quite high. Therefore, the tax benefits of converting your existing home to a rental property will be low, and, as stated, eventually you will lose the greatest tax benefit of all—a capital-gains tax-free sale of a principal residence. If you really believe the area you live in will be an ideal rental-property location, it might be best to actually sell your principal residence, tax-free, then buy another property just like it in the same neighborhood to use as a rental property. By doing so you reset the cost-basis of the structure, increase your depreciation write-off, and therefore increase your tax benefits while still retaining the tax-free sale of your principal residence.

This strategy may not work equally well in all states. For instance, if you live in a state (like California) where your lower property taxes are reset higher when you sell your existing home and buy a new one, you may find the increase in property taxes offset some of the higher depreciation benefits. However, in states where property taxes are the same for existing homes and newly purchased homes you could literally sell your primary home tax-free, buy the house next door, rent it out, and be tens of thousands of dollars ahead.

Buying Property through Your IRA

Another way to acquire rental property is to buy it through your IRA. You can broaden your portfolio by using an IRA to purchase raw land, houses, condos, commercial properties, and even mort-gage loans. This isn't for everybody, but with foreclosed homes selling at dimes on the dollar, residential real estate can some-times be had at a bargain by savvy investors holding cash. And cash is the best way to acquire property in an IRA. Even if the IRA can put the required 20 percent to 30 percent down, lenders may want to charge a higher interest rate on a loan because it's a loan to an IRA, not to a person. Furthermore, any capital gain attributed to the debt financing is subject to income taxes at the IRA level, then taxed again when the funds are withdrawn from the IRA. Properties purchased for cash don't have this so-called unrelated debt–financed income.

An important caveat: Homes purchased with IRA funds can't be used for personal purposes. Nor can personal funds be used to pay for repairs, taxes, and the like. The IRA will need to have other cash to be able to pay for the ongoing costs of operation. The IRS looks askance at self-dealing and what it views as schemes designed to pull money out of the IRA without paying taxes. For instance, a parent's plan to buy a condo in a college town for a child to live in rent-free for four years probably isn't going to fly. You won't be able to put a piece of property that you currently own into your IRA. And the couple who through an IRA buy a time-share they use a few weeks a year will be out of luck.

Any violation of the rules could result in the tax man coming after the buyers for immediate payment of taxes and penalties on the entire IRA account value. Still, purchasing a steeply discounted property for cash can be a good strategy for these uncertain times, especially for retirees with a long-term mindset and whose fixed-income investments are paying paltry yields.

You most likely won't be able to buy real estate with your basic IRA. You'll need to open a *self-directed* IRA (either a traditional IRA or a Roth), and those come with their own complex rules. For starters, you must find an independent custodian administrator to make the acquisition. The custodian holds title to the property in the name of your IRA. The IRA will pay a percentage of the asset value to have the account serviced, and that can amount to a big chunk of change. Those fees vary widely, so be sure to get a complete list before hiring such a firm. You also must figure out a means to manage the property—either by yourself, or through a property manager, or a limited-liability company. (I recommend a LLC and a property manager for maximum asset protection.)

When you set up a self-directed IRA account with a custodian, you transfer assets from brokerage firms holding existing IRA funds. Then income from the property flows back into the retirement account. That income can be directed into all manner of investments typically held within an IRA, be they stocks, bonds, mutual funds, or money-market accounts. And eventually, the account holder may be able to reap the potential appreciation of the underlying asset—the property—that the IRA owns. What's more, proceeds from selling an IRA-owned property roll back into the IRA without facing capital-gains taxes.

So if you're tired of being limited to the typical lineup of stocks, mutual funds, and CDs that most brokerages allow you to buy in your IRA, creating a self-directed IRA might work for you. But beware: You must follow the letter of the law or face IRS penalties. Further, unlike a run-of-the-mill IRA that's invested in stocks and bonds, a self-directed IRA that holds real estate requires considerably more work on your part and arguably entails more risk.

If you don't know much about real estate and aren't prepared to do a lot of due diligence, don't attempt this. Sure, you can lose money in stocks, too. But they're at least liquid. It's much tougher to extricate yourself if you get into a jam with real estate.

So you've got to know the market and the competitive forces. You've got to know your comfort level with risk. And you've got to have the financial wherewithal in your IRA to withstand market downturns. If you're not rock-solid on any of those counts, you might be better off investing in REITs or mutual funds that specialize in real estate.

If I haven't scared you away and the prospect of owning real estate in a self-directed IRA still seems like a good idea, be sure to build a solid team of specialists to work with, likely including a financial planner, a real estate broker, an attorney, an accountant, and a title company.

A Final Word

As the title of this chapter says, play it smart when it comes to personally-owned real estate. I sometimes shudder when I get calls to my radio show from listeners wanting to aggressively use their home equity to buy more real estate. Or, even worse, to borrow against their homes to buy stocks, especially within life insurance policies or variable annuities. That's not only risky, it's usually a very bad use of leverage because the growth of the insurance policy or the variable annuity is stunted due to the drag of mortality and expense charges.

An individual really must have staying power—a good job, lots of expertise, and quite a bit of cash in the bank—and a big dollop of luck to successfully pull off those kinds of deals. Because while leverage (borrowing) can make you money, leverage—as we've seen so dramatically in the past few years—can also take you down, way down.

Before taking money out of your home or out of your retirement accounts to invest in real estate or anything else, be sure to do the math. If the deal doesn't pencil out without assuming continued escalation in stock or real estate prices, back off. At the end of the day, you know, there are worse things than having a lot of equity in your home.

CHAPTER 9

Give Uncle Sam His Fair Share—But *No More*

"Next to being shot at and missed," somebody once said, "nothing is quite as satisfying as an income tax refund." I agree. In fact, I'm a stickler when it comes to not paying unnecessary taxes. Taxes detract from your returns. Taxes directly reduce spendable income, and most people probably are paying several thousand dollars more in taxes each year than they should.

What's more, there's every reason to believe that higher taxes await us. The recession and bailout have pushed the federal deficit to unheard-of levels. How much higher taxes go will depend on the shifting political sands, but it's widely believed that stiffer tax bites are in the offing, especially for those with higher incomes.

While you can't control how well an investment will do, you *can*—with planning—get a measure of control over your tax bill. Yet, for all we complain about taxes, most investors spend little time doing much about minimizing them. So in this chapter we're going to look at ways to easily reduce and, in certain instances, avoid taxes, all done legally.

I have no sympathy for unscrupulous promoters who set up tax shelters to help people illegally evade paying income taxes. Such con artists should be put in prison. It's important to understand the difference between legal and illegal ways to lower your tax bill and, thus, to be able to tell the difference between being helped or being scammed.

You already know that the government gives us quite a few opportunities to legally reduce our taxes. For example, tax-advantaged retirement accounts—such as IRAs and 401(k)s—do that as does the mortgage-interest deduction and the capital-gains exclusion on your principal residence discussed in the previous chapter. You can save for college tax-free in a 529 plan. You can deduct stock losses (up to a point) as well as deduct property taxes, business expenses, and charitable contributions. You can take medical and dental expense deductions if they rise above a certain level. You can do tax-free property exchanges, and . . . well, the list is long.

But here are a few other techniques I think you should definitely know about.

Tax-Free Municipal Bonds

A bond is a loan. If you make a loan to a corporation, the interest you receive is taxed at ordinary income rates. A municipal bond, or "muni," is a loan to a state or local government. When you make such a loan, the interest may be federal income tax-free and perhaps state tax-free as well.

The higher a person's tax bracket, the greater the incentive to invest in a muni. Granted, the pretax yield for most bonds will trump a muni. But investors may be willing a swap a little yield for a better net after-tax return.

So when should you favor a municipal bond over a taxable bond? As a general rule if you are in the 15 percent federal bracket you're better off with a taxable bond. Once you hit the 25 percent bracket, tax-free bonds tend to make more sense. The best way to determine which bond, taxable or tax free, is best is to understand how to determine the taxable equivalent yield (TEY) of the tax-free bond or bond fund. The taxable-equivalent yield tells you what you would have to earn on a taxable bond to break even after taxes with a municipal bond.

The way to figure your TEY is to take the tax-free yield and divide it by 1 minus your tax bracket. For example, let's say that you have a municipal bond trading at par (not at a premium or a discount) that matures in 10 years that pays a 5 percent annual return. Let's also assume you are in a 25 percent tax bracket. If you divide the 5 percent yield by the number 1 minus your tax bracket (1 − .25 = .75), you end up with 6.67 percent (5 percent divided by .75). Thus, if you have a taxable bond maturing in 10 years with similar credit quality paying more than 6.67 percent, then it probably makes more sense to consider buying that bond instead of a tax-free bond.

When buying tax-free bonds, you also need to know if the bonds carry any exposure to the alternative minimum tax. (The AMT is a tax calculation that adds certain tax preference items back into adjusted gross income.) If the bonds do up your exposure to the AMT, you should avoid them unless you receive tax counsel before buying them.

Be aware also that putting muni bonds in a retirement account is a really bad idea. A retirement account already provides tax protection, so you're squandering the benefit that comes from owning a muni.

Tax Management of Stock Portfolios

There's a lot you can do to keep taxes to a minimum on your stock and bond investments. For starters, try to avoid the short-term capital-gains tax that's levied on impatient investors who dump a profitable security before the end of a year and a day. Plus, you can sell your losers to offset your taxable stock gains. Similarly, you can choose mutual funds that are tax-managed or consider index funds or exchange-traded funds that are inherently tax-efficient because there's minimal trading by their managers. And, of course, when you leave a job, resist the temptation to cash out your 401(k) or other workplace retirement accounts. Cashing out if you're below age 59½ will likely bring taxes and penalties, and, what's more, you'll lose out on years of compounding and won't have the money when you'll really need it in retirement.

Real Estate

Investment real estate can be an excellent tax shelter that can increase your spendable income as well as increase your net worth as the property appreciates. Mortgage interest, property taxes, maintenance, repairs, even your travel to check out your property may be tax deductible.

In addition, you can depreciate the improvements on your property over a number of years. For example, if you buy a residential rental property for $1 million and the land cost is $300,000, you can depreciate $700,000 over a 27.5 year period. That gives you an annual write off of $25,455 every year for the next 27.5 years. This deduction is in addition to the write-offs mentioned above. Thus, even after you recognize the income you receive from rents, your write-offs with this depreciation deduction are likely to exceed your income. You'll like that feeling when your accountant files your taxes and you show a tax loss, even though you've actually put money in your pocket.

However, you are phased out of the tax benefits once your adjusted gross income (AGI) exceeds $150,000. So if you are a high-income earner, your tax benefits like depreciation may have to be suspended until you ultimately sell. At that time the suspended losses can be used to offset capital gains, so you still receive a benefit but may have to wait a while.

You can also own vacation property and get some tax benefits. For example, if you own a rental property that can be rented year-round, you may be able to treat it as a rental property for tax purposes and still use it for your own vacations. To do so, there are some specific rules you must follow.

The most important one is the 14-day rule. If you occupy the rental property for *more* than 14 days per year or 10 percent of the rentable days, (if it's a seasonal rental, it may not be available to rent all 365 days; thus, you must use the 10 percent rule), then you can prorate the expenses of the rental property. Direct rental expenses (like advertising) are 100 percent deductible. However, you cannot show a negative return (as you can with a true investment property). If the pro rata rental expenses are greater than the total rental income, you cannot use that "loss" to offset other income, not even from other rentals. But you can prorate the expenses, including depreciation, as long as you don't go negative. However, if you use your vacation property for *less* than two weeks per calendar year, your vacation property will qualify as a rental with all of the associated tax benefits, and you don't need to prorate the expenses.

The opposite of the 14-day rule can also create some tax-free income for some lucky residents. For example, my home is in San Diego, California, not too far from the world-famous Del Mar Race Track. In the summer, horse-racing aficionados, owners, trainers, and big-money gamblers come from all over the world to watch their favorite horses run and enjoy the summer in beautiful San

Diego. Many of these individuals are wealthy VIPs who want to rent an entire house for a week or two.

This type of short-term rental situation is also quite common around several of the big national golf tournaments where homeowners will lease out their entire house for big bucks during the course of a four- or five-day event. I've been told that during the racing season at Del Mar, I could charge rent of upwards of $2,000 per night for my home. If I do that for 14 days and not an hour more, I could pocket $28,000 of tax-free income. That's right! Totally tax free! Follow the rules, and your home and/or vacation home may be a great tax shelter.

Roth Conversion

The Roth IRA, as you may know, is one of the best deals in retirement planning. You put after-tax money in, and it grows tax-deferred and that growth can be withdrawn tax-free, provided the account's existed for five years and you're at least age 59½.

What's more, Roths don't require distributions starting at age 70½ as do traditional IRAs. And your heirs won't owe income tax on their required-minimum withdrawals. Meanwhile, all monies not withdrawn continue to accrue tax-free benefits for your ultimate beneficiary.

Until now, though, income limits and other rules have prevented many investors from enjoying the Roth's many advantages. But the year 2010 gives more people access to this retirement-savings vehicle, including a tax break that may make it advantageous for you to convert some or all of your traditional IRA to a Roth.

Many people previously just made too much money to use Roths. You couldn't contribute to a Roth if your modified adjusted gross income (MAGI) was $120,000 or more ($177,000 for marrieds filing jointly). And you couldn't convert a traditional IRA's assets into a Roth if your household's MAGI exceeded $100,000. (Plus, a married person filing separately was prohibited from converting, no matter what his or her income.)

But in 2010, two big changes took place:

1. Income limits on conversions disappeared permanently. Anybody—even spouses filing separately—will be able to convert retirement assets to a Roth IRA, though they'll owe taxes

on the amount converted. (Income limits on contributions remain in effect.)

2. If you convert in 2010, you can spread your tax bill over two years. You won't need to pay the first installment until 2012, when you file your 2011 tax return, and you can pay the balance when you file your 2012 return the following year. Of course, you can choose to pay all the taxes when you file your 2010 return if that works better than spreading it out.

While you must pay taxes on the entire amount you convert, the lower your account value—and most are lower after the 2007–2008 plunge—the smaller your tax bill. And you can convert as much or as little as you like.

Whether converting makes sense for you depends on a lot of factors. If you're in, let's say, your forties or younger, there's more logic in converting than if you're older. After all, you probably don't have much in your IRA yet, so the tax pain should be minimal, and you have a number of years to compound your Roth tax-free.

Another good conversion candidate would be someone who was, say, a high-income earner during his or her career but who's now living frugally on Social Security and investment income, and has a large, yet-untapped IRA. That person is a good bet for conversion because that IRA is going to be kicking out RMDs at age 70½ and later. And when it does, the retiree could shoot back up into the top tax brackets. So she should consider using up the lower income-tax bracket levels now by converting some of that traditional IRA to a Roth each year.

If you expect to leave your IRA to your heirs, a conversion might also make sense. That's because converting a regular IRA to a Roth reduces your ultimate taxable estate since paying the tax now shrinks your net worth and avoids a potential double tax (income and estate tax) after you die. Thus, the savings to heirs can be sizable.

Also, one of the most onerous and least-understood taxes is the one you pay on your Social Security payments once your MAGI exceeds certain limits. Because the income you take from a Roth doesn't even show up on your tax return (unlike tax-free muni bond interest), by blending your income from traditional and Roth IRAs, you may be able to eliminate or greatly reduce the income taxes you pay on your Social Security.

No one knows what future tax laws will be. But, as I said, with government's huge budget deficits comes the likelihood that tax rates will rise. Thus, future tax-free income becomes especially alluring. In short, you pay lower taxes today to avoid what may be higher taxes tomorrow.

What's the best way to take advantage of these rule changes? First, understand you don't need to convert your entire IRA in 2010. You can do it in chunks (though 2010 is the only time you'll be able to pay the taxes in two increments). If you have a traditional IRA made up largely of pretax contributions—such as a 401(k) rollover—your tax bill could be steep. But a tax professional may be able to help you figure out how much you can convert within your current tax bracket each year without bumping yourself into a higher one.

It's important that you pay the taxes on a Roth conversion with money from outside your IRA. You don't want to pay your taxes with money taken from your IRA because that will greatly reduce the future growth of the Roth. And if you're under 59½, you could also get socked with a 10 percent federal penalty (plus possible state penalties) for withdrawing IRA assets at the time of conversion.

Is it possible to convert, then change your mind? Yes, you can reconvert—it's called a "re-characterization"—a Roth to a traditional IRA, although that isn't common. Most people who make the initial conversion—once they get over the shock of that initial tax hit—are pleased. However, you may discover after the fact that you were ineligible to convert or that a Roth conversion caused you to move into a higher tax bracket, and so the conversion is inadvisable. In that case you can reconvert, but it must be done by October 15 in the year following the year of conversion.

These 2010 changes will allow many people to sleep better knowing they can't be touched by future tax increases. Further, by letting retirees who rolled over their 401(k)s into IRAs to convert to Roths, the changes also will give those investors more flexibility to keep taxes low in retirement.

But I've simplified the rules here. Be aware that these conversions are governed by IRA tax law that can be brain-numbingly complex. One misstep can mess up your nest egg big-time or cause you to pay more tax than you otherwise might have. My suggestion? Seek out professional advice.

Incorporating Your Business

Self-employed individuals pay more in taxes than those employed. That's because the self-employed must pay both the employer and the employee share of the Social Security tax and Medicare premium. For example, an employee who is paid a salary of $80,000 per year will pay 7.65 percent of his pay or $6,120 every year in Social Security and Medicare tax. The employer must also pay an additional 7.65 percent match to the system. Self-employed individuals are both the employer and the employee. Thus, they must pay both halves of the self-employment tax (Social Security tax and Medicare premium) or a total of 15.3 percent. That's a full $6,120 more than an employee earning the same amount.

In addition to paying the extra self-employment tax, a self-employed person is usually responsible for paying 100 percent of his benefit costs such as health insurance, medical reimbursements, retirement plans, and disability insurance. Can a corporation help? Maybe. If you're self-employed, consider switching from a sole proprietorship to a different type of entity, such as an S-corporation or a C-corporation.

An S-corporation is a standard corporation that has elected to opt for a special status with the IRS. This status provides many of the benefits of partnership taxation while at the same time giving the owners limited liability from creditors. Its income is not taxed; instead, the income, or loss, is applied pro rata to each shareholder and appears on her tax return. (This concept is called *single* taxation. If a corporation is taxed as a C-corporation, it will face double taxation, meaning both the company's profits and the shareholders' dividends will be taxed.)

The primary benefit of an S-corporation is the ability to pass through cash dividends and not have to pay Medicare premiums (2.9 percent) and, depending on your salary, Social Security tax (12.4 percent). For example, the self-employed individual who earns $80,000 a year and takes a $60,000 salary out of the S-corp and a $20,000 dividend would save the entire 15.3 percent on $20,000—or $3,060 annually—in Social Security and Medicare taxes. S-corp owners can also gift shares of stock to children, grandchildren, and other relatives, and by doing so shift income to those who perhaps are in a lower tax bracket.

Keep in mind the IRS will look closely at how much salary versus how much in dividends are passed through. The owners' compensation must be "reasonable" relative to how much of the work and profit they're responsible as opposed to how much profit other employees generate. (See a CPA before you decide.)

A C-corporation is a tried-and-true method to protect your personal assets from potential judgments against your company. However, as noted, you're taxed on corporate profits as well as shareholder dividends. On the other hand, a C-corporation also has fewer restrictions than an S-corporation on the number of owners as well as citizenship and residency requirements. There are some great tax benefits afforded to C-corps that are not available to S-corps and Limited Liability Companies (LLCs). For example, a C-corp can take tax deductions for disability insurance, some term-life insurance, medical reimbursement plans, flexible spending accounts, and so on. The rules are complicated, but the savings can be substantial. Again, seek out competent help before you act.

A LLC is a hybrid combining some of the best features of a corporation and a partnership. The primary characteristic it shares with a corporation is limited liability; the primary characteristic it shares with a partnership is the availability of pass-through income taxation. It's often more flexible than a corporation and is well-suited for companies with a single owner.

It's the entity of choice when holding investment real estate. Lawyers often advise clients to form multiple LLCs when they have multiple properties, placing a single asset within each LLC. Assets within the LLC aren't protected from lawsuits from, say, tenants and creditors, but the members of the LLC can't be held personally liable for claims against them resulting from a lawsuit for something that happened at that property, unless that lawsuit was the result of the LLC owner(s)' negligence. Thus, it's recommended that LLC owners subcontract as much as possible and not perform services (such as electrical construction and the like) that could cause them any personal liability.

While S-corps distribute profits pro rata based on ownership, LLCs can distribute profits based on formulas established by the owners. Also, other advantages of LLCs include flexibility in how the profits are distributed; no meetings or minutes are required; and all losses, profits, and expenses "flow through" to the individual members, avoiding the double taxation of paying corporate and individual tax. All 50 states allow for the formation of LLCs. You need to file articles of organization and an operating agreement, which is akin to corporate bylaws or partnership agreements.

However, it's rare that I recommend an LLC to operate a business. Usually a corporation makes more sense, especially if there's just one owner or if profits are to be divided equally among the shareholders. That's because there are few, if any, tax reasons for setting up an LLC.

The biggest advantage of setting up an operating business as a LLC comes if it's a second business and you are already receiving a salary from another job in excess of the Social Security wage base. This way the LLC gives you some liability protection and won't lead to a doubling up on Social Security and Medicare taxes.

As you can see, corporate-tax planning can be quite complex. A competent CPA, tax lawyer, and financial planner can help you navigate through these murky waters. Such good planning can make the end result quite profitable.

Tax-Credit Investing

Many older investors have large IRAs, pension plans, or annuities that may or must be withdrawn and are taxed at hefty ordinary-income rates.

One potential solution is to look for certain tax-credit investments or those with substantial first-year deductions, such as low-income housing tax credits or oil and gas drilling programs. These investments promote affordable housing for the elderly or poor and encourage exploration and energy independence. They may also allow investors to effectively convert some or all of their taxable retirement money into a tax-free Roth IRA, with the tax owed on the distribution offset by the tax credits or tax deductions available from the tax-favored investments.

Low-income housing tax credits were created about 25 years ago by Congress. One way to qualify for the tax credit is by directly building, buying, or renovating apartments to rent to low-income people. But more commonly, investors pool their money in a limited partnership and receive tax credits that lower their federal income taxes each year for the next 10 to 12 years.

A key point is that a tax *credit* is a lot more beneficial than a tax *deduction*. (Credits cut your tax bill outright. Deductions merely lower your taxable income.) So getting a tax credit is almost like getting a tax-free check. But calculating the maximum tax credit you can take each year is pretty complicated and depends on your tax bracket, so you'll want to work with a financial planner or tax specialist who knows his way around this kind of tax shelter.

In a drilling program, investors get to deduct approximately 85 percent of their initial investment in the year they make it. That's because oil wells are a depleting asset and aren't expected to produce forever. But with today's technology, an experienced company may be able to produce oil or gas for many years into the future. And after that 85 percent first-year write-off, the returns could be quite competitive. A $20,000 investment could produce a $17,000 tax deduction that could offset $17,000 of taxable income on a Roth conversion.

Also, let's say you've got a substantial traditional IRA from a 401(k) rollover or one that you've built up over the years. Using a tax-credit program, you can take money out of your IRA each year and use the tax credit to offset the tax. So it's like a tax-free distribution from your IRA. You can then convert that distribution into a Roth and let it grow tax-free. Because there are no distribution requirements on a Roth, you can decide to let the growing sum sit and appreciate for your heirs . . . or you can spend it as you wish.

What's more, you could get a further payback from, say, the low-income property you invested in. If, unlikely as it seems, the partnership eventually sold the property and got nothing—in effect, bulldozed it—you would have still have gotten your tax credits, which would probably amount to about a 4 percent to 5 percent tax-free rate of return. And if the property appreciated nicely, you might get a return of 8 percent to 10 percent or more after taxes.

So in the worst-case scenario, you would have performed a useful social service while making about the same as you'd likely get from a tax-free municipal bond. But in the best case, you could receive about double what a tax-free muni pays. But, more important, by using the tax credit in concert with a Roth conversion, you could build up a tax-free nest egg.

As I said, though, with any investment, risks exist. That's why with these types of investments individuals must meet minimums for income and net worth. Further, keep in mind these are illiquid, long-term investments, and the income may vary over time. In drilling programs, for instance, income in the early years may be quite competitive but usually dwindles as the years go by. Any income and capital-gains payoffs from a tax-credit program may be more than a decade away, and neither are guaranteed. You shouldn't invest any money that is needed for cash flow because in a tax-credit program cash flow is likely to be nil. Rents may barely cover debt and operating expenses in a low-income housing program, and in an oil and gas partnership, the income could start out in the teens but diminish to the single digits in a few short years.

In addition, you need to be careful whom you choose as a partner. The firms you select should have a track record for bringing their respective properties to market and being able to comply with the complicated federal rules. But for the right person, tax credits and oil and gas partnerships can be potentially a lucrative and socially beneficial strategy, especially when coupled with a Roth conversion.

Choosing Smart Location of Assets

Different assets create differing tax liabilities. So deciding wisely where to put those assets is one of the simplest ways to raise your returns. In fact, one study by professors Robert Dammon and Chester Spratt of Carnegie Mellon and Harold Zhang of the University of North Carolina concluded that you may boost your returns by as much as 15 percent to 20 percent over time by getting the right investment in the right account. Here's why: Bonds pay regular interest, which is taxed at ordinary federal income-tax rates as high as 35 percent. By contrast, stocks don't generate taxes until they're sold, at which time the profits are usually taxed at 15 percent if they've been held for more than a year. And some stocks pay "qualified" dividends, which also are currently taxed at a maximum of 15 percent. (The 15 percent capital-gains rate is likely to become 20 percent when the "Bush" tax cuts expire in 2011. The 15 percent dividend rate is also likely to revert to ordinary rates that year.)

With the tax rates on stocks so much lower than on bonds, it makes sense to keep your bonds in a tax-deferred account, such as a 401(k) or an IRA. That way, the interest payments don't generate an annual tax bill. Stocks held inside a tax-deferred account lose the tax advantage of the 15 percent tax on long-term capital gains and dividends. Yet many investors place their retirement-fund money and their personal money in stocks without regard for which accounts receive the best tax treatment.

They could come to regret that because money put into a retirement account gets a tax break today, but when you start taking that money out in retirement, you'll pay ordinary-income rates. That'll turn long-term gains that would have been taxed at today's 15 percent rate into a tax bill of up to 35 percent. If you live a high-tax state—like Illinois, New York, or California—this distinction becomes even more important. Capital-gains tax rates are commonly expected to increase to 20 percent in the future, and ordinary income-tax rates also may be rising even more steeply. So this strategy works now and in the future.

Thus, a good general rule might be: Place your most tax-inefficient investments (bonds, bond funds, and some real-estate investment trusts, or REITs) in your tax-deferred accounts. Put the most tax-efficient ones (stocks, ETFs, and tax-managed stock funds) in your taxable accounts.

But, as with all matters financial, it's not quite that simple. For starters, putting fixed-income assets into a tax-deferred account means you're going to give up some of growth potential of the retirement vehicle. After all, those bonds aren't likely to appreciate the way stocks might be expected to. Further, it's counter intuitive—many people just reflexively put their most speculative stock investments in their retirement account so they can grow without taxation. And they *could* grow tax-deferred . . . until the investor withdraws some of those retirement savings and faces a big tax hit.

Each investor's situation is different, so there is no universal answer about where to hold assets. But in all cases the ultimate goal is the highest after-tax rate of return.

What to do? Here are my suggestions:

Take it slow. If you start selling stocks (especially those held less than a year) and appreciated bonds willy-nilly, you're going to incur massive taxes. A better idea would be to review your situation. Then add any new investments in the right place, especially if you're already retired or nearing retirement. It's the young and middle-age investors who will benefit most by a switch, but even they need to be mindful of unintended consequences.

Choose placement carefully. Because a Roth IRA allows you to withdraw money in the future with no tax consequences, use it whenever possible, especially for bonds and REITs. Place individual stocks and directly owned real estate that you plan to hold for a long time in your taxable accounts; hold shorter-term stock investments in your tax-deferred accounts. Place stock funds with low turnover ratios—say, below 20 percent annually—in the taxable account and those with higher turnover rates in tax-deferred accounts. Put bonds and bond funds in a retirement account— and REITs, too, because REIT dividends aren't eligible for the qualified-dividend tax treatment.

However, some REITs—in particular, certain nontraded REITs— work well in either taxable or tax-deferred accounts. That's because the dividend yield on nontraded REITs is usually higher than on many bonds. So they work well in an IRA and may get significant depreciation write-offs, making them excellent income vehicles in a taxable account.

Plus, understand that additional tax-wise reasons exist to put the right investment in the right kind of account. Stocks and mutual funds that appreciate in taxable accounts receive a step-up in cost-basis when you die. This lets your heirs receive those assets without tax consequences. It's nice to know that at least some of your assets will grow tax free for your heirs.

Thus, if you bought a property or stock for, say, $100,000 in a taxable account, and it grows to $500,000, your heirs receive that $500,000 income and capital gains tax-free. Were that same $500,000 a distribution from a tax-deferred account upon your death, the beneficiaries might need to pay as much as $200,000 (or more in some states) in federal and state income taxes.

Furthermore, capital losses incurred within your IRA or 401(k) are forever lost. But losses incurred in a taxable account may be used to offset ordinary income (up to $3,000 a year) as well as future capital gains. So putting the right kind of assets in the right kind of account can give you an added edge.

A Final Word

The government gives us quite a few chances to legally reduce our taxes—and we should take advantage of those opportunities, doubly so given the likelihood that higher taxes are in the offing.

Tax-free municipal bonds, real estate, and, of course, retirement savings plans (especially Roth IRAs) are obvious possibilities. But don't neglect to check out other avenues, such as incorporating your business, tax-credit investing, and choosing the most tax-advantaged accounts to house your investments.

PART IV

LIVE HAPPILY EVER AFTER

10

Craft a Workable Withdrawal Strategy

I read somewhere that 90 percent of mountain-climbing accidents happen on the *way down* the peak. That may be an apt metaphor. Amassing retirement savings is, for many of us, a long, hard, uphill slog. But if you make a mistake on the uphill grind, you've still got job income coming in regularly and perhaps time to recover. However, run into a problem as you descend life's slope—say, a market that drops 50 percent in a year—and you could end up a financial fatality if you're not well-bucketized.

With the demise of traditional pensions, not to mention paltry savings levels and ever-expanding life spans, many Americans run the risk of seeing their money disappear before the end of their retirement. In fact, according to a 2008 study by Ernst & Young, nearly three out of five middle-class retirees will likely run out of money if they maintain their preretirement lifestyles and don't reduce spending by at least 24 percent.

Of course, reducing spending is not the only factor in the equation. Other variables include when you choose to retire, how much of your income you annuitize, at what age you elect to collect Social Security, what you do with your home, the way you allocate your assets (i.e., your *Buckets of Money* plan), the taxes you pay, and what strategy you have for withdrawing the money you need. In this chapter we'll look at ways that you might draw down your money without scrambling your nest egg.

Too few people know—or think much about—how to plan their investment withdrawals during retirement. Surprisingly, less than half—47 percent—of workers say they or their spouse has even tried to calculate how much money they'll need for a comfortable retirement, according to the Employee Benefit Research Institute. Yet time, the rate of inflation, and expected returns loom much larger in retirement than when you were working. When you were on the job, for example, a couple of bad years of investing could be overcome by adding to your savings or by working longer.

Once retired, though, you'll be withdrawing money in both good years and bad. So you'll need to manage those reserves wisely by maximizing earnings and reducing taxes.

Buckets of Money is a sound, conservative strategy that helps you avoid the common mistake of having either too little exposure to stocks (thus, lacking protection against inflation) or too much (making you overly vulnerable to market whims). But it's not a guaranteed money machine; it still needs to be managed prudently.

Beware of Averages

So when the time comes to plan your withdrawals, beware of averages. Averages—such as the stock market's long-term average annual gain of 10 percent—are helpful, but they can be hugely deceiving. The future is never exactly like the past. In truth, there are few "average" years, and variables abound—including how long you will live, the market's rise and fall, and the pace of inflation.

When you look at returns over, say, 50 years, the ups and downs sort of balance out. But when you start pulling out money in retirement, those ups and downs really matter. Let's say you have a $600,000 stock portfolio. You know the stock market grows long-term an average of more than 10 percent a year. So you might figure you can withdraw $60,000 a year and still keep $600,000 in your account.

But let's say in that first year the market dips 20 percent (a relatively modest decline by recent standards), and your total falls to $432,000 (deducting your $60,000 plus a 20 percent loss on the remaining $540,000). If the market and your account bounce back 20 percent the following year, the *average* market gain/loss for the past two years is 0 percent. But your account is at only $446,400 after you take out another $60,000. Despite what the averages say is a break-even couple of years, you're down $153,600 that you may never get back. In fact, if the market has several such bad years while you're still taking out 10 percent, you could go broke in a surprisingly short time!

Further, the sequence of the returns also matters. Whether the up years come at the beginning, middle, or end of your retirement years makes a big difference. For example, retire just before a bull market and you may live well and pass on a handsome sum to your heirs. Retire just before a bear market and with the same nest egg, same spending rate, you could possibly outlive your money. Again, that's because you're going to be drawing down on a shrinking amount.

In short, real life is more chaotic than your pocket calculator indicates. So you need to work carefully with your financial planner on various scenarios that anticipate a few shocks along the way.

Here are some suggestions to take into that meeting:

- **Assume you'll live to 100.** That's the conservative tack to take.
- **Run several projections,** including some with very conservative returns so you get an idea of the range of possible outcomes. Do the calculations year by year with actual returns rather than the average return for the period. (If your advisor is not a certified *Buckets of Money* specialist, ask her to use something called "Monte Carlo simulation." This takes into account a number of random-performance scenarios and gives you the probability of success or failure. With a properly implemented *Buckets of Money* plan, we look at 15- to 25-year horizons and, thus, are less concerned about year-to-year market fluctuations.)
- **Expect a long-term return of no more than 8 percent on your stock** investments after you retire. (If that turns out to be low, you can attribute the jump in value to your brilliance as an investor!)
- **Get the right mix.** Ask your planner to show you how. By adjusting the mixture of stocks, bonds, cash, and real estate in your portfolio, you can affect the probability that your money will last as long as you do. Then choose a risk factor that's comfortable for you.
- **Withdraw no more than 4 percent per year** of your diversified portfolio. Consider pulling out less in bad years, or at least,

foregoing the usual inflation boost. (More on this later in this chapter.) This won't produce a fixed income but it should help prevent you from running out of money.

- **Tax-manage your portfolio.** Work with your planner and respect her judgment. But make it clear you'd rather be safe than sorry.

Obviously, a key in all this is to hire a really sharp, talented advisor. You need someone who understands you, your goals and objectives. And preferably one who has an excellent grasp of the *Buckets of Money* strategy. (Go to www.BucketsOfMoney.com to find a certified advisor.) That kind of knowledge, training, and flexibility counts for a lot. In fact, in some cases it can even make up for investment underperformance.

Pitfalls Abound

Our legal and tax system features what are probably too many retirement plans burdened with too many rules. Take, for instance, our mind-boggling alphanumeric stew of retirement plans, each with its own regulations. There are, to name just a few, traditional IRAs (deductible and nondeductible), Roth IRAs, 401(k)s, 403(b)s, 457s, SEPs, Keoghs, SIMPLE IRAs, and even Roth 401(k)s. And our tax system makes understanding them tougher than it ought to be.

Indeed, pitfalls are plentiful for those who don't understand the sometimes complicated rules of retirement accounts. Mistakes can be costly. To take just the simplest example, let's say that a 54-year-old retires and transfers a lump sum from her 401(k) to a bank savings account. She could suffer a major tax penalty and lose as much as a quarter or more of her life savings because of this one uninformed decision. (That transfer, unless it was made directly to an IRA in a timely fashion, would be subject to federal and state tax and a 10 percent federal penalty tax.)

The truth is, most folks aren't aware of the importance of planning for how to receive cash during their retirement. They've spent decades accumulating wealth but haven't thought much about converting those savings to retirement income. One study by ING's U.S. financial services found that almost 70 percent of 50- to 70-year-olds had no plan in place for their "retirement paycheck"—that is, how they're going to convert their savings into a lasting income stream.

Making this change is easier if you start planning for the transition well ahead of time. It's easier with some lead time, for example, to pay off credit cards, car loans, and other debts, which should be a priority before you retire. And, of course, it goes almost without saying that you shouldn't be taking on any new debt.

Getting Set Up

To put first things first, make sure that you handle your 401(k) correctly when you retire or otherwise leave your employer. In general, you can do five things with those retirement savings: You can (1) cash out, (2) leave the money in the plan, (3) roll it over into an IRA, (4) roll it over to a new employer's plan, or (5) convert all or part of your retirement savings to a Roth IRA.

If you cash out and terminate employment in the year you turn age 55 or older, you won't be hit with any penalty taxes. But if you take the money and run, as many do, and you're under age 55, you'll be hit with a big federal penalty (and maybe a state penalty, too) as well as income taxes, not to mention missing out on the benefits of your money compounding tax-deferred. So that's not smart.

A big benefit of rolling over the 401(k) balance into an IRA is that you'll have more investment options than in a 401(k) plan. So if, for example, you want to buy CDs, individual stocks or bonds, real estate, or mortgages, that can be done easily and effectively in an IRA. However, most 401(k) plans offer strictly stock and bond mutual funds. Also, by rolling over your 401(k) into an IRA you can consolidate all your wayward retirement accounts in one place. But be careful how you do this rollover. It's best to have the money transferred directly between financial institutions so you don't touch it.

You also could choose to leave your 401(k) with your old employer or roll it over into your new employer's plan. Either choice would make sense if you love the prescreened group of investments offered by that plan, making it a little easier to keep track of your money. But that selection varies from company to company and tends to be pretty skimpy at smaller employers. And if you leave your account with your old employer, make sure that you know about any rules that may apply to the 401(k) accounts of departed workers and how they'll affect your heirs if you die.

IRA Rollover

For most people, establishing a rollover to a traditional IRA is the best option. That's because your money grows faster than it would if you had cashed out the 401(k), paid the taxes and penalties, and put what was left in a taxable account. But, still, many choose to cash out their 401(k)s to buy a new car, a new kitchen, or a European vacation. Long after the thrill of that purchase has waned, though, they may be feeling the shock of the tax-and-penalty bite—and wondering how they're going to afford to retire.

You can establish an IRA rollover account at just about any financial institution. But again, I want to emphasize the importance of doing this carefully. Don't have the check made out to you. Instead, have it made out in the name of your IRA and sent directly to the IRA custodian. Depositing it directly into the IRA rollover account minimizes costly complications, such as the mandatory withholding of 20 percent of any distribution made payable to an individual.

With either an IRA or a 401(k) rollover, you *may* start withdrawing amounts as early as age 59½ without penalty. And you *must* begin such withdrawals no later than the year after you turn 70½—otherwise, you face monetary penalties. Of course, those withdrawals will be taxed at your ordinary income-tax rates. (Roth IRAs also allow you to begin withdrawing your earnings tax-free at 59½ as long as you've had the Roth for five years. But there's no mandatory withdrawal at 70½ or any other age, provided you didn't inherit the Roth from a nonspouse. That's one big reason why Roths are more desirable for certain individuals. Another is that withdrawals are potentially tax free.)

Required Minimum Distributions

So how much do you need to withdraw? The required minimum distribution (RMD) in the year you attain age 70½ (and later) will be the total of your account balances divided by the distribution period calculated by the IRS. In its Publication 590 (see www.irs .gov), the IRS sets out three different tables to be used to determine that divisor. Under the most common, the Uniform Lifetime Table, for example, a 70-year-old would divide his retirement account balances by 27.4, meaning that a $100,000 balance would require a withdrawal that year of $3,650.

These rules can trap unsuspecting seniors. Many, for instance, get tripped up during the first couple years of having to take a distribution. In some cases they fail to take the RMD, saying that they don't need the money. (They may not, but the IRS—which has deferred taxes all those years—still wants its payback.) In other cases, retirees use the wrong year-end account balances or the wrong life-expectancy factors. If you mess up, you will not only pay ordinary income tax on the distribution, but you'll also get stuck with a 50 percent penalty on what you should have taken out but didn't.

How can you avoid this? Check and double-check the life-expectancy factor and year-end account balance. Plus, in most cases, you should really consult a knowledgeable financial advisor.

Adding to the necessity of working with an expert is the fact that the other tables come into play when, for example, you're married to someone more than 10 years younger than yourself and you've named that spouse as a sole beneficiary. (The effect is to make the required minimum payouts smaller.) If that sounds like you, you'll definitely want to get a financial advisor to help you calculate the withdrawals.

And it really gets dicey when deciding which set of rules to follow if you inherit a retirement plan. Further, the rules vary, depending on whether the owner died before or after beginning minimum distributions and whether the beneficiary is the spouse or a nonspouse. So, if your situation is even a little bit out of the ordinary—or even if it's as ordinary as apple pie but you're financially challenged—find yourself an experienced, competent advisor and come up with a withdrawal system that works for you *and* the IRS.

Drawing Down Your Total Retirement Resources

Once retired, you'll need a strategy that includes withdrawing at least the minimally required amounts from traditional IRAs and 401(k)s. Understand, of course, that every person's situation is different, and that a required minimum distribution from your tax-advantaged retirement accounts is only that, a *minimum*.

The IRS does require you to take out at least the minimum once you turn age 70½, whether you need the money or not. (If you're still employed and own less than 5 percent of the company, you don't have to take mandatory withdrawals from the company 401(k).) But the government doesn't care if you take the money as a yearly lump sum or a steady amount each month. Further, the IRS doesn't care if you own just one IRA and draw down on it, or if you have several and drain a little from each of them monthly or yearly or whenever. It also doesn't care if you draw out more than it requires you to. And it doesn't care what you do with the money you withdraw from your IRA—you can spend it or reinvest it in a taxable account.

However, it does care if you have different types of accounts—such as a 401(k), a 403(b), and certain other kinds of retirement plans that have specific RMDs that may not be satisfied by an IRA withdrawal. In other words, a retiree with an IRA, 401(k), and 403(b) will be required to take three separate RMDs (one from each) whereas an owner of three IRAs can satisfy the RMD with just one distribution from any one or combination of the three.

More? And in What Order?

As I say, you must take out the minimum, but you may well want or need to take out more. How much more? Well, that's something your advisor—after looking at your other retirement resources—can help you figure out.

Your advisor also should be able to help you draw down as much money as required to meet your basic needs but not so much that you run out of cash in your sunset years. She will look at the big picture: How much income can you expect to get from a pension, stock options, a part-time job, Social Security, personal savings, or perhaps an expected inheritance? And how much can that income be expected to grow during your retirement?

I believe that a realistic rule of thumb—confirmed by numerous academic studies—is that most people shouldn't withdraw more than 4 percent of the balance of their total retirement resources every year. (That's a *real* 4 percent, meaning that it should be increased each year by the previous year's inflation rate to help you retain the same purchasing power.) That 4 percent gives you the best shot at not outliving your assets.

Which raises a related question: How much of those retirement resources should be in stocks and real estate? (Unlike bonds, stocks and real estate may grow in value, making up some of the depletion as you withdraw money for income.) You may have heard the axiom that says your exposure to stocks should equal no more than 100 minus your age. In other words, if you're 60, you shouldn't have more than 40 percent of your resources in stocks. Indeed, that may have been a reasonable rule generations ago when life expectancies were shorter, but it's certainly not very scientific.

Obviously, the greater allocation you have in stocks and real estate, the more growth potential—and also the more downside risk you'll have. If you follow my *Buckets of Money* strategy, your asset allocation will match your future need for income with a time horizon. For instance, we know that stocks are risky in the short run, but if left alone, with dividends reinvested for 15 years, you're likely to have a positive return. In fact, the worst 15-year period in history for stocks produced a positive return. So conservative investors may want to design their *Buckets of Money* strategy with the stock buckets having a 15-year minimum-time horizon. More aggressive investors or younger retirees may want to go with a 10-year stock bucket, while those faint-hearted about stocks may prefer a 20-year strategy.

Indeed, this is something else you should seriously discuss with your advisor. But the truth is, a lot of people are too conservative with their money. They *under*estimate their life span, and they *over*estimate how much of their nest egg they should keep in fixed-income assets.

An Example

Here's an example that I often use: If you had $1 million and invested it all in bonds at 4.5 percent interest, you'd get $45,000 a year and, of course, at the end of, say, 25 years, you'd still have your million bucks.

Or, you could divide that million into two piles. One pile, let's say $731,000, you invest at 4 percent, and spend it down to almost zero over 25 years. That would also give you $45,000 a year every year for 25 years, the same as you would have gotten with the all-bond portfolio.

Meanwhile, what happens to the other $269,000? Well, you could have invested it in stocks and, based on historical data, you probably could have done pretty well. (Burton Malkiel, a Princeton University professor and the respected author of *A Random Walk Down Wall Street*, says that the *worst* 25-year period since 1950 for domestic stocks as measured by the S&P 500 was about a 7.94 percent rate of return.) So let's suppose you stuck that $269,000 in stocks and did only as well as the worst quarter century since the year I was born. At the end of 25 years, you'd have $1.8 million in stocks, $800,000 more than you started with—and you would have still enjoyed your $45,000 a year. And that's calculating the worst 25-year period since 1950. If your stocks grew at, say, 9 percent, you'd end up with $2.3 million and could leave your heirs more than double what you started with. And if stocks grew at their historical 10 percent return, that $269,000 would have grown to almost $3 million—almost three times what you started with.

This example is akin to a highly simplified version of the whole *Buckets of Money* approach: Spend down part of your money from safe accounts to live on while putting the rest into growth investments that you won't need to touch for a long time. Understand, the point of the example is not that stocks will grow at some predictable rate but that there's a downside to being too conservative. Putting all your wealth into fixed income may not be the smartest thing to do, especially with inflation potentially looming after the government's recent large-scale borrowing and printing of money.

When's the Greatest Need?

When figuring out how much income you're going to need in retirement, you probably ought to take out more income in the early years. Retirement planning traditionally has assumed that a person retains the same lifestyle throughout retirement, but some research now suggests that spending tends to decrease with age. One study in the *Journal of Financial Planning* showed that spending in practically every category—from housing to entertainment—declined with age (the one big exception: health care).

So this raises the possibility that, rather than the inflated 4 percent withdrawal previously discussed, you could withdraw a higher percentage of your savings in the early years of retirement and moderate the annual inflation adjustments. But, of course, as we've seen, many variables exist, including projected life span and stock/bond mix. Also, the kind of insurance you buy to help cover rising medical costs and nursing-home care will definitely figure into this equation. (This is why I recommend you consider a long-term-care-insurance policy.)

Your future spending pattern is something worth devoting some time to with your financial advisor. On the one hand, the few thousand dollars extra that you might withdraw could be what puts the quality in your "quality of life"—like that extra vacation with the grandkids or that newer-model car. On the other hand, you can't go back and unspend in your later years if you take too much out to begin with. For my part, I'd lean toward being conservative, especially at first.

Keeping Taxes Low

The order in which you draw down your retirement money will dramatically affect your retirement income. The common belief is: "Defer, defer, defer your taxes for as long as you can. Live off of your taxable savings and don't tap into your IRAs until you absolutely must at age 70½." (This mantra—like many financial truisms—is good advice for some people and foolish for others.)

So the accepted order of battle for tax-efficient withdrawals is this: taxable accounts first, then tax-deferred accounts (such as IRAs and 401(k)s), and, finally, tax-free accounts (like Roths). But I think, depending on your tax bracket and other factors, it's often a good idea to draw in varying proportions from all three. That way you can seek an optimal blend of taxable and tax-free or tax-deferred money, and thus control your tax bill. Your financial advisor should be able to help devise such a plan. And it's why most *Buckets of Money* plans have several buckets, some for taxable money and some for tax-deferred money.

In short, deferring the withdrawal of IRA money accounts always makes sense—*except* when it doesn't. For example, it may not make sense if you can take money out in a low tax-bracket now instead of a higher bracket later. Take a married couple, age 62, with $50,000 in a money-market fund for emergencies as well as $250,000 in CDs. They have another $250,000 in stocks in an IRA. In addition, they receive $26,400 yearly in Social Security benefits and have a pension that pays them $18,000.

According to conventional wisdom, they should live off of the income from their $300,000 in bank accounts (the $50,000 in emergency money plus the $250,000 in CDs) and continue to invest their IRA in stocks until they are forced to take minimum IRA distributions at age 70½.

Their income and tax situation now looks something like this:

Now

	Receive Yearly	Amount Taxable
Pension	18,000	18,000
Social Security Income	26,400	5,100
$50,000 Money Market (at 3 percent)	1,000	1,000
$250,000 CD (at 4 percent)	10,000	10,000
$250,000 IRA (stocks)	0	0
Total Income	$55,400	$34,100
Minus Write-offs/Personal Exemptions		−18,700
Taxable Income		$15,400
Tax due		$ 1,540

On the surface this looks great. The IRA isn't paying out yet—it's compounding tax-free as IRAs are supposed to do. Meanwhile, the couple is in the 10 percent tax bracket and paying only $1,540 in taxes each year. Even if they bucketize the $250,000 in personal assets, their tax situation will not change dramatically.

Assuming their stocks earn 8 percent over the next eight years (when the couple turns 70½), their IRA will be worth something on the order of $465,000. Based on the IRS tables, they will need to make a minimum distribution of about $16,900 in the first year and increasing every year thereafter.

Thus, if they remain on the present course, their situation would look something like this in eight years (assuming, for simplicity's sake, no change in Social Security, pension benefits, or tax rates):

At Age 70½ Remaining on Present Course

	Receive Yearly	Amount Taxable
Pension	18,000	18,000
Social Security Income	26,400	18,825
$50,000 Money Market (at 2 percent)	1,000	1,000
$250,000 CD (at 4 percent)	10,000	10,000
$465,000 IRA (stocks)	16,890	16,890
RMD (required minimum dist)		

	Receive Yearly	Amount Taxable
Total Income	$72,290	$64,715
Minus Write-offs/Personal Exemptions		−20,900
Taxable Income		$43,815
Tax due		$ 5,735

So, adding that $16,900 IRA distribution will cause their tax bill to almost quadruple. They'll pay federal taxes of $5,700 vs. a tax of $1,500 that they were previously paying.

But let's take a look at how they might do better with a smart *Buckets of Money* strategy. What they could do is:

- Put the $50,000 emergency fund in a tax-free money-market fund. That'll reduce the interest, of course, but also will contribute to reducing the tax bill.
- Convert the $250,000 in CDs to a well-diversified, tax-managed, all-stock portfolio with the objective of long-term growth subject to long-term capital-gains tax when sold. They would call that their Bucket 3.
- Convert the IRA stock assets into safe investments funding Buckets 1 and 2 (e.g., bonds and CDs) and take the income from the IRA to meet their needs, at least to the extent of using up their 15 percent tax bracket. (It's good to use up that money now because otherwise the income could be received in the 25 percent bracket later.)
- So under a scenario in which we tax-manage the portfolio but keep the income roughly the same, the couple's situation for the next eight years would look something like this:

Now . . . If Tax-Managed/Bucketized

	Receive Yearly	Amount Taxable
Pension	18,000	18,000
Social Security Income	26,400	7,235
$50,000 tax-free money market (at 1 percent)	500	0

Continued

	Receive Yearly	Amount Taxable
$250,000 Tax-Managed Stock Portfolio (Bucket 3 figuring 1.5 percent dividend partially reinvested)	3,750	0*
$250,000 IRA CDs/bonds (at 4 percent) (Buckets 1 and 2)	10,000	10,000
Total Income	$58,650	$35,235
Minus Write-offs/Personal Exemption		−18,700
Taxable Income		$16,530
Tax Due		$ 1,650

* Taxed at 0 percent (under current law as of 2010).

So though the couple still has roughly the same amount to spend ($58,650 vs. $55,400), they have positioned themselves better for that time when they must draw down their IRA. They also effectively used the 10 percent and 15 percent tax bracket to their advantage in structuring their buckets.

So with this new, tax-managed structure, their situation at age 70½ (when they must start taking distributions from their IRA) will look like this:

At Age 70½ If Tax-Managed/Bucketized

	Receive Yearly	Amount Taxable
Pension	18,000	18,000
Social Security Income	26,400	9,870
$50,000 Tax-Free Money Market (at 1 percent)	500	0
$457,000 Tax-Managed Stock Portfolio (Bucket 3 figuring 1.5 percent annual dividend partially reinvested to keep cash flow steady)	6,855	6,855
$250,000 IRA CDs/Bonds (at 4 percent) (Buckets 1 and 2) RMD (required minimum dist.)	10,000	10,000
Total Income	$61,755	$44,725
Minus Write-offs/Personal Exemptions		−20,900
Taxable Income		$23,825
Tax Due		$ 2,735

Note that the IRA distribution could be reduced as the dividend on the stock portfolio increases. This is good because the couple meets its income needs without additional distributions—and thus, without additional taxes. The bottom line? They'll pay less than half the tax ($2,735 vs. $5,735) per year when they turn 70½ than if they hadn't restructured their income.

The point is that it's crucial to study the impact of taxes on each bucket. A further point, of course, is that it makes sense to have a professional advise you before setting up any buckets plan. That's because, as in this case, there are taxes on Social Security, potential taxes upon death, and ordinary income versus capital-gains issues that really must be addressed. The right advisor and a good plan can increase your rate of return by simply shuffling your assets to the proper buckets and applying tax management.

And that's my point: While many financial journalists espouse the philosophy of do-it-yourself investing, I tend to take a different approach. The tax savings above more than pay for a little tax advice and rarely will you get that type of advice from those who write generically about finance.

A Few More Thoughts about Stocks

I've spent a lot of time in this book covering real estate. That's because it's an asset class conspicuously absent from most Wall Street asset-allocation models. But as we've learned, real estate is not only an important asset class but an imperative one. Similarly essential are stocks and other equity alternatives that have the potential to grow over long periods. The stock market is covered continuously by financial pundits and talking heads on the business channels, news networks, magazines, even radio talk shows. As a result, most of us feel we have a decent grasp of the stock market, and if not, plenty of web sites exist that will dole out tons of advice, some for a fee and some for free. Unfortunately, none of the pundits, software, or websites can predict the future direction of the stock market accurately on a consistent basis. Not the newsletters, not the talking heads, not even the most revered gurus can tell you what is going to happen tomorrow based on what happened yesterday. If they could, their track record would be significantly better. As previously stated, according to cxoadvisory.com, the predictions of the top market gurus they track are correct only 46 percent of the time. Flipping a coin, you could get to 50 percent and not have to buy their services.

This is why you need a *Buckets of Money* strategy—a strategy that delivers a safe and secure income stream while the riskier investments, like stocks and alternatives have an opportunity to grow over long time periods. And I *do* mean long, 15 to 25 years long. With that kind of time horizon you should be able to withstand even the grizzliest of bear markets.

The "Lost Decade"

You may have heard someone say, "Buy and hold is dead," or "Diversification or asset allocation no longer works." This is simply not true *if* you have the appropriate time horizon. Also keep in mind that those promulgating such nonsense want you to trust their judgment of when to buy and when to sell. But when the gurus are right less than 50 percent of the time, I don't like the odds.

You've probably also heard about the "lost decade" and how stocks from the years 2000 through 2009 produced a negative return. That's true over that particular 10-year period, one of the worst decades in history. But it doesn't worry "bucketeers" because the *Buckets of Money* strategy doesn't expect stocks to become totally liquid in 10 years. In fact, as previously discussed, one could spend Bucket 1B, Bucket 2, and Bucket 3A before needing to begin tapping into Bucket 3B, the stock-and-alternative investment bucket. In most instances using very conservative growth estimates for all of the buckets, this strategy of sequentially liquidating each bucket while leaving the stock investments alone actually allows Bucket 3B about 25 years to grow before it needs to be tapped.

You'll recall that, according to Burton Malkiel's *A Random Walk Down Wall Street*, the worst 25-year period for stock returns since 1950 is just short of 8 percent. So let's take a look at the lost decade in the context of a 25-year time horizon. Going back to 1985 through 2009, the prior 25-year period, stocks as measured by the S&P 500 earned an average 10.14 percent per year. That's using an unmanaged index, no market timing, no hedging, no added alpha—nothing! Just the value of the stock market over 25 years. Incidentally, even the 15-year period from 1995 through 2009— which includes the "lost decade"—still produced a return of about 7 percent for the broad stock market as measured by the S&P 500. So it was hardly a lost decade and a half!

No Need to Gamble

What all this proves is you don't need to be a timer, a trader, or a gambler with your stock bucket. If you simply buy, reinvest the dividends, and hold, you still should end up with far more money 25 years from now than you have today if you're properly bucketized and if you manage to keep your withdrawal rate to a reasonable percentage.

That doesn't mean I don't believe active management can't add value. Two of my favorite money managers whom I've used personally over the years have proven their stripes very well over the so-called lost decade. For example, my very capable domestic money management firm I use has been able to best its comparative benchmark (the Russell 1000 growth index) by about 9 percent per year compounded for the 10-year period ending on Dec. 31, 2009. That's quite a feat because the Russell 1000 returned –3.99 percent during the same period.

Also the very fine international management company I use produced a 10-year return of about 13 percent versus their benchmark (the MSCI EAFE Index), which earned 1.58 percent. Interestingly enough, both money managers at some point underperformed their respective benchmarks during the 2008–2009 meltdown but still their 10-year track record is significantly better than their respective index. Had I bailed out on them before the upswing in their performance, I would have lost out. But when you have talented money managers with solid track records, chances are they will recover and continue to outperform.

These are just two examples of many managers I know well and have used over the years. I'm sure there are many others. However, my point is that even if you don't have confidence in your ability to select money managers and instead choose to simply buy various index funds and hold on for dear life during the bad times, the market tends to mend itself over time. With a 15- to 25-year holding period, stocks will most likely be the best-returning asset class in your portfolio.

So how should you allocate your Bucket 3B, the stocks-and-alternatives bucket? Percentages vary among many mangers and advisors. Clearly, in addition to the large-cap blue chip names, you should have a strong commitment to international and emerging market stocks, small- and mid-cap stocks, and commodities such as precious metals. I also like pure-play timber (that's the trees, not the lumber or saw mills). It has actually produced the best return at lower risk than practically all other assets over the past 20 years.

The key, of course, is creating your asset allocation and sticking with it over long time horizons. This asset allocation can be accomplished using unmanaged index funds or exchange-traded funds (ETFs), mutual funds, or separate account managers, or a combination of all of the above. I prefer to use a core strategy consisting of a broadly diversified portfolio and then add some separate account money managers running concentrated portfolios attempting to add value (alpha) by good stock selection and overweighting or underweighting certain sectors based on their research. For example, say my $1,000,000 buckets plan called for $400,000 in equities and alternatives. I divvy up it as you can see in the Suggested Allocation shown in Table 10.1.

In this allocation I would hire at least two, possibly three, institutional money managers (large-cap, domestic, small-cap, and international), then fill in with mutual funds and ETFs and so on for the smaller accounts. Further, I would rebalance and/or value-average every year or two to stay consistent with my asset-allocation model.

One thing I would *not* do is make any attempt to time the market or use any type of technical analysis. It's been proven in finance labs all around the world time and again that luck plays a more significant role than reading the tea leaves or following charts or

Table 10.1   Suggested Allocation

Large Cap Domestic	35%
Growth & Value	
Mid-Cap Domestic	15%
Growth & Value	
Small Cap Domestic	10%
Growth & Value	
International	20%
Emerging Markets	10%
Commodities	10%
Oil, Timber, Precious Metals, and so on	

graphs over long periods. That doesn't mean I'm opposed to do-it-yourself stock picking. If you enjoy it and do your homework, you may be able to do very well.

But just keep in mind the information you're using to make stock selections is already well known by all of the professionals that manage money for a living. So your chances of doing significantly better at the same level of risk are probably less than you may think. For those bent on doing it themselves, my suggestion is to build your broad portfolio first using professional money management and then carve off a piece of the portfolio that you manage personally. As you do better and better, transfer more and more under your control. But always remain diversified and always use at least three or four different money managers. That's because even the best method will blow up occasionally and you don't want all of your eggs in that one basket.

And that, of course, is among the beauties of the *Buckets of Money* strategy. It's the smart, safe way to retire because your eggs are spread over a number of baskets, or buckets, and are diversified both as to the types of investments and time periods over which they'll be held. As a result and as I mentioned at the beginning of this book, as you grow older, you may see others needing to make do with less and less. But you, having mastered the strategy, will potentially be growing stronger and more secure.

You may choose to set up the allocation yourself, or you can decide to rely on a trained *Buckets of Money* specialist. (For a free *Buckets of Money* analysis, see www.BucketsOfMoney.com.) Whichever route you choose, here's wishing you good investing, good luck, and—as the Epilogue suggests—a very good life.

A Final Word

We spend a lot of time and energy figuring out how to accumulate retirement assets, but few us spend enough time planning how we're going to draw that money down once we're retired. Yet managing those savings wisely can maximize earnings, reduce taxes, and help assure a comfortable retirement.

My suggestion: Work closely with a financial planner, take a conservative tack (such as assuming you'll live to 100 and projecting no more than an 8 percent annual return on your stocks), and keep your withdrawal rate at a low 4 percent or even less in bad years.

Epilogue

KEEP YOUR EYE ON ENJOYMENT

Have we hit bottom? Is the nascent recovery "V-shaped," "U-shaped," or a double-bottomed "W-shaped"? Will the market retest its lows? Will personal bankruptcies climb and employment fall? Is the dollar imploding? Will gold hit the stratosphere?

I don't know the answers to those and many other pressing economic questions. What I *do* know is that—in the long term—they're probably not all that pressing. What I truly believe is that if you proceed diligently and intelligently in the direction of your dreams, you've got a decent shot at achieving them. And those dreams should include, but not be limited to, your financial well-being.

I may be among the few financial commentators in stressing this, but I think you need to keep this dollar stuff in perspective. Sure, "Money is coined liberty," as Dostoevsky wrote, and I hope *Buckets of Money* will give you money and liberty in abundance. But you also need engagement and connection with people and pursuits. If you're never rich in anything but friends, family, and worthwhile things to do, you're still pretty rich.

Happiness is a state of mind, not a state of wealth. "Success is getting what you want," Warren Buffett tells us. "Happiness is wanting what you get."

For me, happiness involves being so deeply involved in the moment that we don't have the opportunity to think about anything but the task at hand. Or, to put it another way: Happiness is probably more a bunch of little, enjoyable moments than a series of really big deals. Life ought to be about more than being shrewd in wealth accumulation.

Columnist Anna Quindlen has urged: "Get a life in which you pay attention to the baby as she scowls with concentration when she tries to pick up a Cheerio with her thumb and first finger. Turn off the cell phone. Turn off your regular phone, for that matter. Keep still. Be present. Get a life in which you are not alone. Find people you love, and who love you."

We should think about the things that truly make a difference in our later years. Things like our health, our spiritual soundness, our relationships with our family and friends . . . and having a plate full of interesting things to do. The true measure of our lives is not what we accumulate but rather who we are and the number of people we bless with our touch.

For whatever they're worth, here are my Seven Rules for an Enjoyable Retirement:

1. **Invest well** . . . in friendship and good times. Doing so will probably be more beneficial for you than investing in pork-belly futures, land in Uruguay, or the latest in German automotive engineering. Needs and expenses have an amazing ability to keep pace with income. So you can decide to make more . . . or, to need less.

2. **Always seek value** . . . in how you use your time. You'll no longer be ruled by the clock. So, provided your health is good, put your emphasis on quality priorities, such as travel, hobbies, family . . . you name it. Think about how you want to spend your time. How would you answer the question posed by poet Mary Oliver, "Tell me what is it you plan to do with your one wild and precious life?" Do you know? Or are you so consumed with projects, deadlines, and acquisitiveness than you haven't given it much thought recently? Each of us has been granted but a brief stay on this little blue ball. How shall we use it?

3. **Spend a lot** . . . less than you earn. Remember Charles Dickens's famous formula: "Annual income, 20 pounds; annual expenditure 19 pounds; result happiness. Annual income, 20 pounds; annual expenditure, 21 pounds; result misery." The secret of happiness is not necessarily found in seeking more but in honing the capacity to enjoy less. Sure, we all must consume to survive, and Madison Avenue is right there, nudging us to do so—buy this status-conferring watch, drive that incomparable luxury car, move into this lavish, prestigious home. But rarely does acquiring things generate the fulfillment we imagine. Money, possessions, luxury—these are not the hallmarks of a life well lived but, at best, merely its byproducts.

4. **Share the wealth** . . . of your abilities. When you give of yourself—
   and not just of your money—is when you truly give. So whether
   you're being a mentor, a docent at a museum, or just handing
   out flyers for a favorite cause, you'll help others and yourself at
   the same time.

5. **Accumulate many** . . . memories, not things. The joy you receive
   in retirement won't correlate directly with how much money
   you have but with how involved you are with other things. A lot
   of us give lip service to the idea that amassing money now will
   allow us later to do what we really want. That may be true . . .
   but not if we keep postponing whatever it is we'd really like to
   do. "A man is a success," Bob Dylan once said, "if he gets up
   in the morning and goes to bed at night and in between does
   what he wants to do."

6. **Compound your interest** . . . in people and the world around
   you. We all recognize that some people get more joy out of
   life than others do. The same is true in retirement. This joy
   doesn't correlate with how much money you have. It cor-
   relates, I believe, with how *involved* you are. Involved with
   your family, friends, country, planet. Involved with trying to
   make life better for others. Involved with physical activity and
   mental stimulation. Involved with romantic love. Involved
   with pets and grandchildren, or with origami, or pinochle, or
   writing, or taxidermy, or raising roses, or anything else that
   interests you.

7. **Bequeath a valuable inheritance** . . . by giving your kids enough
   to do something but not enough to do nothing. Without a
   doubt, your greatest legacy will be your example.

Much of this book has been aimed at seeking to help you stave
off fears that you won't have enough money in retirement. I hope
I've helped allay those concerns. But I also want to be clear that
money should represent not just security, but freedom and an
expanded appetite for life.

To me, good health and time with family are the building
blocks of happiness. Wealth, on the other hand, doesn't necessarily lead to contentment because people with more money just want
more things. When we put money in its appropriate place, we find
that the rest of life sort of falls into its rightful place. We put our
money in service to ourselves instead of being in service to it.

Again, Buffett: "Of the billionaires I have known, money just brings out the basic traits in them. If they were jerks before they had money, they are simply jerks with a billion dollars."

As I sometimes like to say, it's important not to confuse being well-off with well-being. "There are no luggage racks on a hearse," the wags tell us. Being successful at retirement doesn't mean ending up as the richest guy in the cemetery. It means living as richly as possible the latter third or so of your life.

In short, happiness is a state of mind, not a state of possessions. The true measure of our lives is not what we achieve—and certainly not what we accumulate—but rather who we are and the number of people we manage to touch.

"The true perfection of man," Oscar Wilde said, "lies not in what man has, but in what man is."

About the Authors

Ray Lucia is one of the nation's leading authorities on financial, tax, and retirement planning. An author, radio-TV personality, keynote speaker, entertainer, and Certified Financial Planner, he is highly qualified to render expert advice to individuals and businesses in all areas of financial planning. Over the course of his 36-year career in financial services, Ray Lucia has helped thousands of individuals invest billions of dollars utilizing his *Buckets of Money* retirement strategy.

He's a nationally renowned and sought-after speaker on subjects such as Social Security, pensions, investments, asset allocation, and taxes. He has trained thousands of advisors and has addressed public audiences all across the country with long-time friend Ben Stein. Unlike many pundits or other radio, print, and television financial journalists, Ray Lucia, CFP has actually built one of the most successful retirement planning organizations in the country. His vast knowledge and practical experience sets him apart from most of his peers.

Ray Lucia and his radio Brain Trust (Rob Butterfield, JD; Rick Plum, CFP; and John Dean) field questions on the nationally syndicated *Ray Lucia Radio Show*, which airs daily from noon to 3 P.M. EST in many of the top markets nationwide. It's been called "the most informative and entertaining show on the radio." Ray Lucia is also a TV personality with both a local (San Diego) and national presence. He has appeared on the FOX News Channel, FOX Business, CNBC, NBC's *The Today Show*, and Bloomberg.

Dale Fetherling has written or co-authored more than 15 nonfiction books. The San Diego-based author and editor also has taught writing and editing at five colleges and universities. Learn more at www.bookspartner.com.

Recommended Resources

Books

Ralph L. Block, *Investing in REITs Real Estate Investment Trusts* (Bloomberg, 2006).

Ronald Cordes, Brian O'Toole, and Richard Steiny, *The Art of Investing and Portfolio Management* (McGraw-Hill, 2007).

Ric Edelman, *Rescue Your Money: Your Personal Investment Recovery Plan* (Free Press, 2009).

Stephen Huxley and J. Brent Burns, *Asset Dedication: How to Grow Wealthy with the Next Generation of Asset Allocation* (McGraw-Hill, 2004).

Raymond J. Lucia, *Buckets of Money: How to Retire in Comfort and Safety* (Wiley, 2004).

_____, *Ready . . . Set . . . Retire! Financial Strategies for the Rest of Your Life* (Hay House/New Beginnings Press, 2007).

Burton Malkiel, *A Random Walk Down Wall Street: The Time-Tested Strategy for Successful Investing* (Norton, 2007).

Jack Marrion, *Index Annuities: Power & Protection* (Advantage Compendium, 2004).

Ben Stein, *Yes, You Can Still Retire Comfortably* (Hay House/New Beginnings Press, 2005).

Larry Swedroe, *Rational Investing in Irrational Times: How to Avoid the Costly Mistakes Even Smart People Make Today* (St. Martin's, 2002).

Web sites

www.aarp.org/money/revmort

AARP's consumer's guide provides a glossary, fact sheet, FAQs, and other resources for understanding reverse mortgages.

www.BucketsOfMoney.com

My web site offers materials to assist with your Buckets planning, including worksheets, calculators, articles, case studies, and my seminar schedule. You can create your unique Buckets strategy.

www.cxoadvisory.com

The CXO Advisory Group LLC provides research and reviews—including evaluation of pundits—designed to aid investing decisions.

http://crr.bc.org

The Center for Retirement Research at Boston College does research into Social Security, employer-sponsored pension plans, household saving, and labor market trends among older workers.

www.ebri.org

The nonpartisan Employee Benefit Research Institute seeks to provide objective data and analysis on health, retirement, and other economic-security topics.

www.finra.org

The Financial Industry Regulatory Authority (FINRA), which oversees brokerage firms and their representatives, seeks to be an advocate for investors. Its site provides information on investing, suggests ways to avoid fraud, and allows users to check on the background of brokers and securities firms.

www.irs.gov

The Internal Revenue Service site includes access to tax forms, withholding calculators, refund information, and explanations of recent tax changes.

www.morningstar.com

A treasure trove of investment news and research, Morningstar is a definitive source for information on mutual funds and ETFs.

www.sec.gov

The Securities and Exchange Commission site allows investors to file a tip or a complaint, check out brokers and advisors, and search for company filings. Also, the SEC's new Investor.gov site is aimed at helping investors avoid fraud.

http://ssa.gov

The Social Security Administration's site allows you to estimate your retirement and Medicare benefits as well as apply for them.

www.reit.com

The site of the National Association of Real Estate Investment Trusts includes REIT news and statistics.

Index